EMPLOYMENT LAW MADE EASY

LAWPACK

Employment Law Made Easy
by Melanie Hunt

First edition 1999
Second edition 2001
Third edition 2002

LAWPACK

76-89 Alscot Road London SE1 3AW
www.lawpack.co.uk
All rights reserved.
Printed in Great Britain

ISBN 1 904053 08 4

Exclusion of Liability and Disclaimer

Table of contents

3   Family-friendly rights 73

4   Discrimination 95

5   Termination of employment 117

Introduction

Few legal fields change as rapidly as employment law. New statutes influenced by case law, economic policy changes, trade union practices, government intervention and the tremendous impact of membership of the European Union and the European Court of Justice all mean that employment law is constantly being tested, reshaped and redefined. The last year in particular has seen a number of developments regarding employees' rights. This in turn affects the relationship between employer and employee and both parties need to be aware of their rights and duties. All employees have a right to know what law protects them in the workplace; and employers must know how changes in the law could affect their companies. The idea of seeking legal remedies through confrontation in the courts for violations of employment law has become increasingly acceptable in recent years.

In 2000 alone there was a plethora of new legislation in the UK, such as Maternity and Parental Leave etc Regulations 1999, the Part-Time Workers (Prevention of Less Favourable Treatment) Regulations 2000 and the Data Protection Act 1998. We are also expecting further new legislation with the Fixed Time Working Regulations (due to be introduced in late 2002) and the Employment Act (due to come into force in July 2002). Much of this legislation is intended to replace the notion of conflict between employers and employees, with the promotion of partnership. Whilst the notion of partnership should be encouraged, the practical effect of the new legislation is to increase individual rights and to place an even greater responsibility on the employer to ensure that it complies with its new 'employee-friendly' obligations. In addition, since 2 October 2000 the Human Rights Act 1988 has been in force, incorporating the European Convention on Human Rights and Freedoms (1993) into English and Welsh law; this is likely to permeate into most areas of law, including employment law. The rights that have most relevance to employment law are: the right to a fair trial, private and family life, freedom of thought, conscience and religion, freedom of expression, freedom of assembly and prohibition of discrimination. The Act is not directly enforceable in proceedings brought against a body in the private sector, but it will have an indirect effect on the outcome because courts and tribunals are obliged to interpret UK legislation so as to conform to the Convention.

Because the growth of email, voice mail and other office-based communications has changed the way people work, the need to monitor employees in the use of such communications has become necessary for employers to run their business. This needs to be balanced against the right of employees to privacy. It is quite possible that the Human Rights Act 1998 will give rise to some interesting issues surrounding the monitoring of telephone calls and email. In the meantime, the Government has moved to address concerns about the legality of surveillance/ monitoring of employees by implementing The Telecommunications (Lawful Business Practice) (Interception of Communications) Regulations 2000.

One of the purposes of this book is to promote good communications in the workplace. It may draw your attention to areas of potential or actual conflict. When they arise disputes can usually be resolved through deliberate, honest negotiation. No employer enjoys having to take disciplinary action – let alone dismiss an employee – because of the sense of failure it frequently brings on both sides. But if dismissal is the only course of action it must be done in a legally acceptable way.

This Made Easy Guide provides a broad overview of basic employment law principles. Employment law is a large subject and inevitably there will be some omissions. However, this Guide will alert you to the conditions, practices, responsibilities, duties and remedies that fall within the scope of employment law, and help you navigate your way through them.

Melanie Hunt
27 June 2002

Important facts

This Made Easy Guide contains the information, advice and example contracts and letters to help maintain employer/employee relations in line with the law and codes of practice. It is intended for use in England and Wales. However, much of the legislation is generally applicable, or is mirrored, in Scotland and Northern Ireland, but readers are advised that practices may vary in these jurisdictions.

The information this Made Easy Guide contains has been carefully compiled from professional sources, but its accuracy is not guaranteed, as laws and regulations may change or be subject to differing interpretations.

Neither this nor any other publication can take the place of a solicitor on important legal matters. As with any legal matter, common sense should determine whether you need the assistance of a solicitor rather than relying solely on the information and forms in this Made Easy Guide.

Recruitment

Chapter 1
Recruitment

Recruitment is divided into two main sections in this chapter: the first on the legal requirements behind recruitment and the second, beginning on page 12, on recruitment guidelines and codes of good practice.

LEGAL REQUIREMENTS

When recruiting staff, it is very important that an employer complies with the legal requirements – in particular relating to discrimination – as laid down in legislation. The legal requirements that are dealt with in this chapter are as listed above.

Discrimination

This chapter deals with discrimination during the recruitment process. Chapter 4 takes a broader view of discrimination in employment, its definition and the legal recourse available to employees who feel they have been unlawfully discriminated against.

No matter whether employers are recruiting through employment agencies, job centres, careers offices or schools, they have a duty not to discriminate. They must neither give instructions nor bring pressure to discriminate.

Discrimination on the ground of sex, race or marital status

It is unlawful for employers to advertise vacancies, select interview candidates or offer employment in a way that discriminates on the ground of sex, race or marital status. An employee or job applicant who feels that he or she has been discriminated against on any of these grounds can raise a complaint with the Equal Opportunities Commission, the Commission for Racial Equality or an employment tribunal.

Exceptions

There are some jobs for which the sex or race of the successful candidate may be a 'genuine occupational qualification' and in these circumstances discrimination in advertisements, in the interview procedure, in job offers, in offers of promotion, training or transfers is acceptable.

(a) **Sex**: A person's sex is a 'genuine occupational qualification' for a job in the following circumstances:

- where the essential nature of the job calls for someone of a certain sex for reason of **physiology** e.g. a female model;

- where it is necessary to preserve **decency or privacy** because the job is likely to involve physical contact with people of the opposite sex in circumstances where those people may reasonably object to the job holder being of the opposite sex, or because the holder of the job is likely to do work in the presence of people who are in a state of undress or are using sanitary facilities and therefore might reasonably object to the presence of a person of the opposite sex;

- where the nature or location of the job means that the job holder must **live in** the premises provided by the employer. Because it is impractical for them to live anywhere else and the premises are not equipped with separate sleeping accommodation or sanitary facilities for men and women, it is unreasonable to expect the employer to equip the premises with such accommodation or facilities;

- where the job is in a **single-sex establishment** or single-sex part of an establishment for people requiring special care, supervision or attention, and the essential character of that establishment or that part makes it reasonable to restrict the job to a person of the same sex as those for whom the establishment (or that part of it) exists;

- where the job is for the provision of **personal services** to people in order to promote their welfare, education or other similar services and those services can most effectively be provided by someone of a certain sex;

- where the job involves **working outside the UK** in a country whose laws and customs are such that the duties could not, or could not effectively be performed by a man (or by a woman);

- where the job is one of two held by a **married couple**.

(b)   **Race**: A person's race is a 'genuine occupational qualification' for a job in the following circumstances:

- where the job involves **dramatic performance** and someone of a particular racial group is required for authenticity;

- where the job involves working as a **model** for producing works of art, picture or film and a person of a racial group is needed for authenticity;

- where the job involves working in a **restaurant** open to the public in a particular setting for which someone of a particular racial group is required for authenticity;

- where the job involves the provision of **personal services** to a particular racial group in order to promote their welfare and those services can be best provided by someone from the same racial group.

Age discrimination

Although there is no express legislation prohibiting discrimination on the ground of age, there is a voluntary code of practice which attempts to tackle the problem of age discrimination. The Government has announced proposals to introduce laws to stop age discrimination, and under European law, this must be implemented by 2006. Also see chapter 4 on age discrimination as unlawful indirect sex discrimination.

Trade unions

It is unlawful for an employer to refuse employment on the grounds of membership or non-membership in a trade union.

Pregnancy

In relation to pregnancy, any decision not to appoint a woman on the grounds that she is pregnant is likely to be found to be discriminatory against sex.

Disability discrimination

It is unlawful for an employer with 15 or more employees to unjustifiably discriminate against a disabled person on the ground of their disability. This law applies in a similar way to the current sex and race legislation at all stages in the recruitment process. Please note that the exemption for employers with less than 15 employees is due to be abolished in 2004, but in the meantime small employers are also encouraged to follow good practice guidelines.

Employee's past criminal convictions

Spent convictions

After a certain period of time, people who have been convicted of criminal offences and who have served their sentences are not under a duty to disclose those convictions to a prospective employer. These convictions are known as 'spent' convictions. If spent convictions are disclosed to prospective employers it is unlawful for them to take the offences into account when considering someone for a job and if they do so they will be guilty of unlawful discrimination. The periods of time (known as rehabilitation periods) depend on the seriousness of the offence and are set out in Figure 1 below. In certain professions, offices and occupations all previous offences must be disclosed regardless of the period of time that has expired.

Sentence	Rehabilitation periods
Imprisonment, corrective training or sentence of detention in a young offenders' institution for between 6 and 30 months	10 years
Imprisonment or sentence of detention in a young offenders' institution for a term not exceeding 6 months	7 years
A fine or the sentence not expressly covered by the Rehabilitation of Offenders Act 1974	5 years
Order for detention in a detention centre	3 years
Absolute discharge	6 months
Conditional discharge	1 year
Probation	5 years
NB For young offenders, periods are usually reduced by half, except in cases of probation	

Figure 1. Rehabilitation periods

Unspent convictions

Job applicants can obtain a document, known as a 'criminal convictions certificate', disclosing any unspent convictions from the Criminal Records Bureau, if required to do so by an employer. The fee for obtaining such a certificate is currently £12. Any employer wishing to use this service will need to register with the Criminal Records Bureau in advance of a check being carried out. Further details are available on the Criminal Records Bureau's website at www.crb.gov.uk.

Employing children and young persons

DEFINITION

A 'child' is defined as anyone younger than the minimum school leaving age. 'Young persons' are defined as anyone over school leaving age but under 18. Young persons are protected by the Working Time Regulations which limits the number of hours young workers may work and provides rules on the daily and weekly rest periods an employer must give to young workers.

No child may be employed:

- if under the age of 13 years;
- during school hours;
- before 7am or after 7pm;
- for more than two hours on any day on which he or she is required to attend school;
- for more than two hours on a Sunday;
- in any industrial undertaking; or
- where they are likely to suffer injury from lifting, carrying or moving heavy items.

A local education authority has powers to supervise the employment of school children in its area and may require particulars about a child's employment. It may prohibit or restrict employment if it feels that the employment is unsuitable, even if not unlawful. A person who wishes to employ a child must obtain a permit from the local education authority.

In addition, the Health and Safety Executive (HSE) provides guidance on the employment of younger workers.

Restrictions on employing women

The following restrictions on the employment of women are for the protection of women and it is lawful to discriminate in employment to comply with these requirements:

- employment in factories within four weeks of childbirth;
- employment in a range of processes involving lead or lead compounds;
- employment in a range of processes in the pottery industry;
- protection from exposure to ionising radiation; and
- employment on ships or aeroplanes while pregnant.

Employment of EU and EEA nationals

The 15 member States of the European Union (EU) are: Austria, Belgium, Denmark, Finland, France, Germany, Greece, Ireland, Italy, Luxembourg, the Netherlands, Portugal, Spain, Sweden and the United Kingdom. The European Economic Area (EEA) comprises EU members plus Iceland, Liechtenstein and Norway. Citizens of the EU and EEA are known as European Nationals and they do not need work permits; they have the right to come to the UK and look for work. Family members of European Nationals also have an automatic right to accompany such European Nationals to the UK. However, if they wish to stay in the UK for more than six months they are advised to apply for a residence permit.

Exception

Member States of the EU are entitled to exclude employment in public service from the general requirements of free movement of labour, and may reserve such employment for their own nationals. The definition of employment in public service in this context is not a question of status of the employee but rather on whether the employee exercises powers conferred by public law or is responsible for safeguarding the general interests of the state.

Employment of non-EU nationals

Someone who is subject to immigration control must obtain a work permit before taking up employment in the UK, unless he or she belongs to one of the categories of people for which this is not necessary. These include:

- ministers of religion;

- representatives of overseas newspapers, news agencies and broadcasting organisations;

- private servants of diplomatic staff;

- sole representatives of overseas firms;

- teachers and language assistants under approved exchange schemes;

- employees of an overseas government or international organisation;

- seamen under contract to join a ship in British waters;

- operational ground staff of overseas owned airlines;

- seasonal workers at agricultural camps under approved schemes;

- doctors and dentists in post-graduate training;

- business visitors admitted by the Home Office;

- Commonwealth citizens with the right of abode and those with at least one grandparent born in the UK.

For further details about applications for work permits contact the Works Permit UK Helpline, listed in the Appendix.

It is a criminal offence (punishable by a fine of up to £5,000) of employing a person without immigration authorisation to work in the UK. An employer has a defence if it can prove that it saw an original of one of a number of specified documents which confirmed that the employee was entitled to work in the UK (see Figure 2 opposite). Employers do not have to check documentation on staff employed prior to 21 January 1997. It is important for employers to adopt procedures which will protect them from prosecution but which also do not breach the race discrimination legislation (see chapter 4). The Home Office has published guidance notes for employers, which are available by telephoning 020 8649 7878.

- Any document containing the National Insurance number of the person named in a document issued by the:

    Inland Revenue
    Benefits Agency
    Contributions Agency
    Employment Service

- A passport stating the holder to be a British citizen:

    having the right to live in the UK
    having an entitlement to re-enter the UK

- A passport issued by, or on behalf of, the UK Government containing a Certificate of Entitlement to live in the UK.

- A certificate for Registration of Naturalisation as a British citizen.

- A Birth Certificate issued in the UK, the Republic of Ireland, the Channel Islands or the Isle of Man.

- A passport or national identity card which describes the holder as a National of the State issuing the documents, that State being a party to the European Economic Area Agreement.

- A passport or other travel document or letter from the Home Office stating that the holder is exempt from immigration control or has indefinite leave to enter or remain in the UK, or has no time limit to stay.

- A passport or other travel document or letter from the Home Office stating that the holder has current leave to enter or remain in the UK and is not precluded from taking the employment in question.

- A UK residence permit held by a European National.

- A passport or other travel document stating that the holder has a current right of residence in the UK by virtue of being a family member of a named European National in the UK.

- A letter from the Home Office stating that the named person is a British citizen or has permission to take up employment.

- A work permit or other document permitting employment issued by the Department for Education and Employment or the Training and Employment Agency or the Training and Employment Agency (Northern Ireland) or the Northern Ireland Social Security Agency.

- A passport stating that the holder is a British Dependant Territories citizen by virtue of a connection with Gibraltar.

Figure 2. Documents as evidence of entitlements to work in the UK

RECRUITMENT GUIDELINES

As well as complying with employment legislation, employers are encouraged to follow good practice when recruiting. The Equal Opportunities Commission and the Commission for Racial Equality both publish codes of practice and recruitment guidelines for employers. Failure to observe these codes of practice does not render an employer liable to proceedings. But, if proceedings are brought in an industrial tribunal under the Sex Discrimination Act 1975 or the Race Relations Act 1976 any relevant provision of either of the codes may be taken into account. Employers are advised to consider their practices carefully at each stage in the recruitment process. These are divided into:

- Advertising

- Selecting and interviewing job applicants

- Choosing the successful candidate

- Making the job offer

Advertising

Employers must avoid biased language in recruitment advertising. Adverts will be illegal if they discourage certain groups (as identified in the discrimination section of this chapter) from applying for the jobs. For example:

'Salesman wanted ...'.

This is an example of gender bias because the word "man" indicates that women applicants will not be considered for the position. The word "salesperson" would be acceptable, or alternatively an indication in the advertisement that both men and women may apply.

'Single professional sought ...'.

This is an example of discrimination on the grounds of marital status and is illegal because the employer is denying applications from qualified married people in favour of those who are unmarried.

In addition to the wording of the adverts, other points to consider, which the codes of practice referred to above recommend, are as follows:

- Always place adverts in publications or areas that are likely to reach both men and women and which do not exclude or disproportionately reduce the number of applicants of a particular racial group.

- Never present men and women in stereotyped roles.

- Be wary of recruiting solely by word of mouth as this may limit members of a certain sex or race from applying.

- If applicants are supplied through trade unions and members of only one sex or a particular racial group (or a disproportionately high number of them) come forward, discuss this with the unions; an alternative approach may have to be adopted.

- Never make the length of residence in or experience of the UK a requirement of the job.

- If a qualification for the job is required, always state that a fully comparable overseas qualification is as acceptable as a UK one.

What should an advertisement include?

It is good practice to prepare a written description for each job title. From this written description an employer may specify the most important duties and requirements of the vacant post in the advertisement as follows:

- the qualifications and experience required;

- any specific skills required;

- experience with specific equipment required;

- the salary and benefits offered;

- the person to contact;

- the required references.

If in doubt about whether the advert is appropriate, ask the personnel department, a legal adviser or someone in a senior position to review it before it is published.

Selecting and interviewing applicants

Selection criteria and/or tests

The purpose of selection criteria and tests is to ensure that an individual has the ability to perform or train for a particular job. The employer should avoid insisting on irrelevant qualifications. Selection criteria and tests should be reviewed regularly to ensure that they remain relevant and are not unlawfully discriminatory.

Once selection of applicants has been carried out letters should be sent inviting candidates for interview and rejecting unsuccessful applicants (see the example letters 1 and 2 at the end of this chapter).

'Dos' and 'Don'ts' when selecting and interviewing job applicants

The following checklist outlines what the employer should and should not do during the selection and interview process:

Do

- process all applications in the same way

- ask questions at the interview which relate to the requirements of the job

- ensure that all employees who come into contact with job applicants are properly trained about legal obligations in respect of discrimination and how to avoid unlawful discrimination

- keep records of interviews showing why the applicants were or were not appointed

Don't

- keep separate lists of male and female or married and single applicants

- ask questions at the interview about personal circumstances such as marital status, children, domestic obligations, marriage plans or family intentions

- make jokes at the interview that are sexist or racist or otherwise biased

Making the job offer

After the selection process, and once a suitable candidate has been chosen, a conditional offer should be made. References should then be taken up and medical examinations should be arranged if required (see the example letters 3–5 on the following pages). If and when the preferred candidate has accepted the offer, rejection letters should be sent to the unsuccessful candidates (see example letter 6).

Example Letter 1
Letter inviting candidate to attend interview

Ace Fabrics Limited

16 Willow Walk, Retford, Nottingham NG6 8WS
Tel: (01777) 121211 Fax: (01777) 121233 Email: acf@uk

Dear *Miss Porter*

Thank you for sending me your application for the post of *Machinist*.

I would very much like to discuss this matter further with you and have arranged an interview at *10am/pm on Tuesday 6 August 2002* at these offices. I should be grateful if you would confirm your attendance.

I look forward to meeting you.

Yours sincerely

John Smith

John Smith
Personnel Manager

Registered Office: 16 Willow Walk, Retford, Nottingham NG6 8WS
Reg. No: England 1212298762

Example Letter 2
Rejection letter before interview

Ace Fabrics Limited

16 Willow Walk, Retford, Nottingham NG6 8WS
Tel: (01777) 121211 Fax: (01777) 121233 Email: acf@uk

Dear *Miss Porter*

I refer to your application for the post of *Machinist* with this company.

I regret that after careful consideration you have not been selected for interview on this occasion as there were other applicants whose experience and qualifications matched our requirements more closely.

However, I would like to take this opportunity to thank you for your interest in our company and I should like to wish you every success in your future job hunting.

Yours sincerely

John Smith

John Smith
Personnel Manager

Registered Office: 16 Willow Walk, Retford, Nottingham NG6 8WS
Reg. No: England 1212298762

1 References are usually taken up at this stage, the offer being made subject to satisfactory references. See example letter 4. A candidate who receives a job offer subject to satisfactory references should not resign from their current employment until all the conditions have been satisfied. In the public sector offers are usually made unconditional only after all conditions are met.

2 Medical examinations of prospective employees are not a legal requirement although employers are recommended to carry them out now that health and safety in the workplace is so important. A prospective employee is not obliged to agree to have a medical examination although if they did refuse it would be reasonable for the prospective employer not to make an offer.

Example Letter 3
Letter of offer of employment

Ace Fabrics Limited

16 Willow Walk, Retford, Nottingham NG6 8WS
Tel: (01777) 121211 Fax: (01777) 121233 Email: acf@uk

Dear *Miss Porter*

Post of *Machinist*

Following your interview at this office on *Tuesday 6 August 2002* I am pleased to offer you the above position with *Ace Fabrics Limited* ("the Company") subject to satisfactory references[1] and a medical report.[2] It is the Company's final decision as to whether such references meet with its requirements. You are advised not to resign from your present position until I have confirmed to you that your references have been received and are satisfactory to us. We will endeavour to obtain your references as quickly as possible.

If you accept this offer of employment, your job will be based at *16 Willow Walk, Retford, Nottingham NG6 8WS.*

Your employment will commence on *Monday 2 September 2002* and the first four weeks will be treated as a probationary period during which time your employment may be terminated by yourself or by the Company on one week's notice.

Your duties and responsibilities will be as set out in the attached job description and you will be responsible to *Mr Brown*.

Your basic salary at the commencement of your employment will be *£13,500 per year* payable monthly in arrears by bank credit transfer on the last day of each month. Your normal weekly hours will be from *9am to 5pm Monday to Friday with one hour break for lunch.*

(continued) ...

Registered Office: 16 Willow Walk, Retford, Nottingham NG6 8WS
Reg. No: England 1212298762

3 Alternatively, these may be set out in an enclosed statement of particulars of employment or incorporated into this letter.

4 Once this offer has been accepted the parties have entered into a contractual relationship and the employer will need to issue either a full contract or a statement of particulars of employment (see chapter 2).

Example Letter 3
Letter of offer of employment (continued)

… (continued)

You will be entitled to *4 weeks* holiday in every year, in addition to the normal statutory entitlement, of which no more than *two* weeks may be taken consecutively. The holiday year runs from *1 February to 31 January.*

The Company will be entitled to terminate your appointment by giving you written notice of *one week for the first two years of service plus one week for every further year of service up to a maximum of twelve weeks.*

You are required to give the Company *one* week's notice of your intention to terminate your employment with the Company.

Your other terms of employment will be provided on your first day of employment.[3]

If you wish to accept this offer of employment I would be grateful if you could confirm your acceptance by signing and returning one copy of this letter in the stamped addressed envelope enclosed.[4]

I do hope that you will accept this offer. In the meantime, if you wish to discuss any aspect of this offer, please do not hesitate to contact me.

Yours sincerely

John Smith

John Smith
Personnel Manager

1 There is no legal obligation to provide a reference although it is rare that an employer or ex-employer will refuse to supply one. If a reference is given, it should be accurate. If it is not accurate the person who gives the reference may be liable to an action for: (a) **defamation** by the subject if the inaccuracy damages the reputation of the subject. The person who gives the reference will not be liable for defamation if they believe the information to be correct and gives it without malice; (b) **negligence** by both the subject and the recipient, both of whom could sue for damages for any financial loss arising out of a negligent reference. Wording may be included in the reference to exclude legal liability as in example letter 5.

2 The request may be for a reference to be given over the telephone and sometimes employers or ex-employers are more willing to give fuller information than in writing. Again, there is no legal obligation to give a reference over the telephone but if it is given, it should be accurate.

3 All references should be marked 'private and confidential'.

4 It is customary to include a stamped address envelope for the return reference. The advantage of this is that the reference is returned straight to the person for whom it is intended.

5 In addition to obtaining references a potential employer is advised to check the prospective employee's qualifications, if possible before the job offer is made.

Example Letter 4
Letter of request for reference[1]

Ace Fabrics Limited

16 Willow Walk, Retford, Nottingham NG6 8WS
Tel: (01777) 121211 Fax: (01777) 121233 Email: acf@uk

Dear Sir

Re: Miss Porter

The above named has applied to us for the position of *Machinist* and has given us your name as a referee.[2]

We understand that *Miss Porter* was employed by you from *2 January 1993 to 2 August 2002* as a *machinist*. We should be grateful if you would confirm that this is the case and let us know whether in your opinion she performed her tasks competently and conscientiously.

We should also be grateful if you would let us know whether you would consider *Miss Porter* a reliable and responsible employee. Could you also let us know the reasons why she left your employment?

We assure you that any reply that you may give will be treated in the strictest confidence.[3]

A stamped addressed envelope is enclosed.[4]

Yours faithfully[5]

John Smith

John Smith
Personnel Manager

Registered Office: 16 Willow Walk, Retford, Nottingham NG6 8WS
Reg. No: England 1212298762

Example Letter 5
Reference letter on employee

FABRIC WORKS LIMITED

Unit 17 Felsham Trading Estate
Bovingdon HP17 2LS
Tel: (01987) 789456
Fax: (01987) 654987
Email: fwl@uk

Dear *Mr. Smith*,

Re: *Miss Porter*

In reply to your request for a reference for the above named, I confirm that *Miss Porter* was employed by this Company between the dates of *2 January 1993 and 2 August 2002* as a *machinist*.

During her employment with this Company *Miss Porter* performed her tasks competently and conscientiously and I consider her to be a reliable and responsible employee. *Miss Porter* left our employment due to redundancy.

This reference is given to be of help to you and in fairness to your proposed employee. It is given on the basis that we accept no legal liability and that you must rely upon your own judgement whether or not to proceed with your proposed employment of this individual. We trust you shall hold this reference in strict confidence.

Yours sincerely

Peter Johnson

Peter Johnson
Managing Director

Registered Office: Unit 17 Felsham Trading Estate Bovingdon HP17 2LS
Registered in England no 123 9876

1 It is a good idea to wait until the preferred candidate has accepted the offer before sending the letters of rejection to the other candidates. Subject to this, it is good practice to notify unsuccessful candidates as soon as possible.

Example Letter 6
Rejection letter after interview[1]

Ace Fabrics Limited

16 Willow Walk, Retford, Nottingham NG6 8WS
Tel: (01777) 121211 Fax: (01777) 121233 Email: acf@uk

Dear *Miss Porter,*

Thank you for attending the interview for the post of *Machinist* at this office on *Tuesday 6 August 2002.*

I regret that after careful consideration your application has been unsuccessful on this occasion as there were candidates whose qualifications and experience matched our requirements more closely.

However, I would like to take this opportunity to thank you for your interest in our company and I should also like to wish you every success in finding a suitable post in the near future.

Yours sincerely

John Smith

John Smith
Personnel Manager

Registered Office: 16 Willow Walk, Retford, Nottingham NG6 8WS
Reg. No: England 1212298762

The employment relationship

2

Chapter 2

The employment relationship

What you'll find in this chapter:

- ➠ General principles
- ➠ Statutory rights of employees
- ➠ Types of contract of employment
- ➠ Terms of contract
- ➠ Variation of contract
- ➠ Staff Handbook
- ➠ Employees and the self-employed

Once an offer of employment has been accepted, the parties enter into a contract of employment, which is the legal basis of the employee/employer relationship. This chapter outlines the main principles of employment contracts which employers need to know in order to avoid legal problems.

General principles

DEFINITION

A contract of employment is generally governed by the same legal principles as any other contract in that there must be:

- an offer;

- an acceptance;

- valuable consideration;

- reasonable certainty in the terms; and

- an intention to create legal relations.

The contract may be oral or in writing or a mixture of the two and is governed by express and implied terms which set out the rights and obligations of the parties. However, employers have a legal duty to issue their employees a written statement of the main terms and conditions under which they are to be employed. This must be issued within two months after the employment begins, but does not constitute the contract of employment. It is merely the employer's version of what he or she believes the main terms to be. The written statement may become a contract of employment but only where the parties have expressly agreed to this. A mere signature by the employee to acknowledge receipt of the written statement does not amount to agreement that the terms are the contract of employment.

In addition to the right to have a written statement issued, employees have further statutory rights, details of which are given below. Subject to these statutory rights, the parties to a contract of employment are free to agree upon any terms they wish.

Statutory rights of employees

An employee becomes entitled to *statutory rights* (i.e. laid down by law) upon entering into an employment contract without any need for the details of these rights to be written into the contract. A number of these rights depend upon the employee having attained a qualifying period of employment. The main rights are described in more detail below.

DEFINITION

1. **National minimum wage** An employee's rate of pay must not be below the NMW. The rate for the NMW is £4.20 per hour before deductions for those aged 22 and above. People aged 16 and 17, those on formal apprenticeships and those working and living as part of a family are exempt from the NMW. There is a rate of £3.60 per hour for those aged from 18 to 21 and for workers in the first six months of a new job with a new employer who are doing specific training. Employees who do not receive the NMW may bring a claim against their employer in the employment tribunal. For more details, and to verify the current rate of

NMW, contact the NMW Helpline on 0845 600 0678 or website on www.tiger.gov.uk.

2. **Equal opportunities** (see chapter 4)

3. **Itemised pay statements** An itemised pay statement must be issued to all employees at the time of payment and must include the following particulars:

    *   gross earnings

    *   net pay

    *   fixed and variable deductions from gross earnings

    *   if the net pay is paid in different ways, the amount and method of payment of each part payment

    Employees may raise a complaint with an employment tribunal if the employer fails to issue a pay statement or if the content is in dispute.

4. **Equal pay for like work** or work rated as equivalent or work of equal value (see chapter 4)

5. **Maternity rights and benefits** (see chapter 3)

6. **Notice of termination of employment**

    Statute lays down minimum notice periods for termination of employment as follows:

    By the employer:

Length of service	Minimum notice period
Less than 1 month	Nil
1 month–2 years	1 week
2–3 years	2 weeks

    and an additional week for each year of continuous employment to a maximum of 12 weeks.

    By the employee: one week.

    The contract of employment may impose a duty to give a longer period of notice.

    See chapter 5 for further details on the recommended procedure for giving notice of termination of employment.

7. **Guarantee pay**

'Guarantee' payments must be made to employees with at least one month's service, when they could normally expect to work but no work is available. Periods when employees are laid off because there is no work available must be agreed in advance to avoid the employer being in breach of contract.

An employee is entitled to a maximum payment of £17 per day for up to 5 days in any period of 3 months where they are laid off. Therefore, the annual maximum is currently £340. See page 70 for an example notice to employees being laid off giving guarantee payments.

An employee may raise a complaint with an employment tribunal if his or her employer fails to pay the whole or part of a guarantee payment to which he or she is entitled. The employment tribunal can award compensation equal to the amount of guarantee payment which it finds due to the employee.

8. **Redundancy pay** (see chapter 5)

9. **Healthy and safe working environment**

All employees are entitled to be provided by their employer "so far as is reasonably practicable" with a safe place to work and access to the place of work, a safe system of work, adequate materials, competent fellow employees and protection from unnecessary risk of injury. Where there are more than five employees employed at any one time the employer must prepare and bring to the notice of its employees a written statement of its policy with respect to health and safety at work.

A model policy, intended for smaller businesses, is available from The Stationery Office but ideally the content of the policy statement should be tailored to meet the employer's particular requirements.

The Health and Safety at Work legislation is too complex to cover in this Guide, but employers should be aware of the importance of fulfilling their obligations. The Health and Safety Commission (HSC) and the Health and Safety Executive (HSE) are both established by the Health and Safety at Work etc. Act 1974 and can provide advice. HSE publishes guidance notes on this subject which are available from HSE Books, listed in the Appendix.

The Working Time Regulations provide for an average 48-hour working week; minimum breaks and 11 consecutive hours rest in any 24-hour period; four weeks' paid holiday and an average 8 hours' work in 24 hours for night workers.

10. **Sickness benefit**

Subject to satisfying certain conditions all employees are entitled to receive statutory sick pay (SSP) from their employers when they are absent from work for four or more consecutive days up to a limit of 28 weeks in a three-year period. Unless the employee has a contractual right to normal pay, SSP is all the employer is obliged to pay him or her during sickness. The model contract included at the end of this chapter provides for normal remuneration for a limited period (see page 53). The current weekly rate of SSP is £63.25, verifiable by contacting the Department of Education and Employment or ACAS (see the Appendix).

Employees are not eligible for statutory sick pay if:

- they are aged under 16 or over 65;

- they have a contract of services which is for a specified period of three months or less and it has not been extended;

- their average weekly pay is below the point at which national insurance contributions are payable (currently £75 per week);

- they have received social security benefit in the 57 days before the first day of sickness;

- they have not yet commenced working;

- they become sick while pregnant during the statutory maternity pay period (see chapter 3);

- they have been due SSP for 28 weeks from a former employee and the last day on which SSP was paid is eight weeks ago or less;

- they become sick during a trade dispute at their workplace, unless they can prove they have no direct interest in the dispute;

- they are in legal custody.

If notified that an ineligible employee has been absent for four or more consecutive days an employer must send a form to the employee within seven days of being notified which explains why SSP is not payable. The employee may then claim incapacity benefit. For expert guidance on all aspects of SSP contact the Inland Revenue helpline on 08457 143143, or obtain a copy of the *Employer's Manual* on SSP (CA30).

11. **Remuneration on suspension on medical grounds**

An employee is entitled to be paid for up to 26 weeks if he or she is suspended on medical grounds in compliance with any regulation or law which concerns the health and safety of workers.

An employee is only entitled to claim a medical suspension payment if he or she has been continuously employed for a period of one month. An employee employed for a fixed term of three months or less or under a specific task contract which is not expected to last for more than three months is not entitled to a medical suspension payment.

An employee will lose the right to payment where:

- he or she is incapable of work by reason of disease or bodily or mental disablement;

- the employer offered the employee suitable alternative employment (whether or not it was work that the employee was engaged to perform) and the employee unreasonably refused to perform that work; or

- he or she failed to comply with the employer's reasonable requirements imposed with a view to ensuring his or her services were available.

The amount an employee is entitled to be paid is 'a week's pay' (or a proportion of 'a week's pay') for every week of suspension. 'A week's pay' is calculated according to statutory rules and is also the basis for the calculation of redundancy payments and unfair dismissal. For an explanation of how to calculate a week's pay, see the Department of Trade and Industry's booklet entitled *Rules governing continuous employment and a week's pay*.

Employees may raise a complaint with an employment tribunal for failure to make a medical suspension payment. Such a complaint must be made within three months of the day on which it is alleged that payment was not made. The tribunal will extend the time limit if it was not reasonably practicable for the claim to be made within three months.

12. **Time off**

    (a)   *Holiday*

        Four weeks' paid holiday.

    (b)   *Public duties*

        An employee is entitled to time off for the purposes of performing his or her public duties. See Figure 3 below for a full list of such duties.

- As a justice of the peace.
- As a member of a local authority.
- As a member of the Broads Authority[1].
- As a member of any statutory tribunal.
- As a member of a board of visitors or a visiting committee.
- As a member of a National Health Service trust, a Regional Health Authority, an Area Health Authority, a District Health Authority, a Family Practitioner Committee or a Health Board.
- As a member of the managing or governing body of an educational establishment maintained by a local education authority or a school council or the governing body of a designated institution or a central institution.
- As a member of the governing body of a grant-maintained school.
- As a member of the governing body of a further education corporation or higher education corporation.
- As a member of a school board or of the board of management of a self-governing school.
- As a member of the board of management of a college of further education.
- As a member of the National Rivers Authority or a river purification board.

[1] An authority with responsibilities for conservation and recreation on the Norfolk Broads.

Figure 3. Public duties that employees are permitted time off to perform

Time off is unpaid and the amount of time off depends upon the employer's business and the effect of the employee's absence.

There is no statutory right to have time off for jury service or attending court as a witness. However, an employer who prevents such attendance would be in contempt of court.

Although there is no legal obligation on employers to pay employees whilst they are on jury service, doing so is conducive to good employee relations. Jurors may however claim an allowance for travelling subsistence and financial loss.

(c)   *Trade union activities, duties and training*

Officials of independent trade unions are entitled to time off with pay to perform duties concerned with the industrial relations in the company and to undergo training. There is also a right to time off to accompany another worker at disciplinary and grievance hearings.

Union members are entitled to time off without pay in order to take part in trade union activities.

(d)   *Elected employee representatives*

An employee who has been elected for consultation purposes for collective redundancies or the transfer of an undertaking is entitled to reasonable paid time off to perform the functions of a representative. They also have the right to paid leave to undergo training.

(e)   *Safety representatives*

Safety representatives who have been appointed by recognised trade unions are entitled to paid time off during working time to carry out their functions and undergo training in aspects of these functions. Representatives of non-unionised workplaces are also entitled to paid time off to carry out their functions and undergo training.

(f)   *Pension scheme trustees*

Pension scheme trustees of the employer's own scheme are entitled to time off during working hours for performing their duties as a trustee or for training in connection with those duties.

(g)   *Maternity leave, including antenatal care*

See chapter 3.

(h)   *Redundancy*

An employee who is declared redundant and has at least 2 years' continuity of employment is entitled to reasonable, paid time off to look for a new job or to arrange training for a new job.

An employee may raise a complaint with an employment tribunal if the employer refuses to allow such time off or fails to pay for it.

(i)   *Parental leave*

Both men and women are entitled to take up to 13 weeks' unpaid leave from work for the purpose of caring for a child for whom they have responsibility. For full details see chapter 3.

(j)   *Time off for dependants*

There is also a new right for employees to take a reasonable amount of unpaid leave to deal with incidents involving dependants; for full details see chapter 3.

13.   **Protected rights on the transfer of a trade or business**

Where a trade or business is transferred from one employer to another, the employees of that trade or business automatically become employees of the new employer, as if their contract of employment were originally made with the new employer. The service is counted as continuous from the date on which the employment commenced with the first employer.

It is beyond the scope of this Guide to cover fully this complex area of employment law, and those who think they may be involved in a transfer of a trade or business should seek professional advice.

14.   **Not to be unfairly dismissed** (see chapter 5)

15.   **Written reasons for dismissal** (upon request)

An employee does not have an automatic right to a written statement of reasons for dismissal. However, if the employee has 2 years' continuous service and asks his or her employer for such a statement the employer must provide one (the rules for assessing what is continuous service are set out in sections 210–219 of the Employment Rights Act 1996).

In practice, it is a good idea to give the dismissed employee the reasons for dismissal in the notice of termination.

16. Written statement of terms and conditions of employment

All employees have a right to be provided with a written statement of the terms and conditions of their employment unless (i) their employment is for a period of less than one month.

The information that the employer provides may be given in instalments but certain items must be given in a single document, described as the *principal statement* (see Figure 4 below). Reference to other documents is permitted only in relation to certain limited matters. As already mentioned the principal statement does not automatically constitute a contract of employment, even if the employee acknowledges receipt of it with his or her signature. To be enforceable, the parties must expressly agree that it is the contract of employment.

Information which must be included in the principal statement:

- the names of the parties;

- the date on which employment began and the date on which any previous employment (with this or any other employer) commenced which is to be regarded as continuous with this employment;

- the scale or rate of remuneration or the method of calculating such remuneration and the frequency of payment;

- any terms and conditions relating to hours or work, including normal working hours;

- any terms and conditions relating to entitlement to holidays, including public holidays and holiday pay (sufficient to enable the employee's entitlement, including entitlement to accrued holiday pay on termination, to be precisely calculated);

- the employee's job title or a brief description of his or her work;

- the employee's place of work, or where the employee is required or permitted to work at various places, an indication of that fact, together with the address of the employer.

(continued) …

Figure 4. Statement of terms and conditions of employment

Information which must be given in writing (but which may or may not be included in the principal statement)

(Where there are no terms to be given under any of these headings, this should be stated.):

- where the employment is not intended to be permanent, the period for which it is expected to continue;

- where the employment is for a fixed term, the expiry date;

- the length of notice the employee is obliged to give and is entitled to receive in order to terminate his or her contract (or reference to the law or an accessible collective agreement);

- rules relating to sick leave, and sick pay (or reference to a document where such details may be found);

- any collective agreements which directly affect the employee's terms and conditions of employment including, where the employer is not a party, the names of the parties;

- details of any pensions or pension schemes (or reference to documents where such details may be found);

- a statement of whether a contracting-out certificate is or is not in force;

- where the employee is required to work outside the United Kingdom for more than one month, the period of such service, the currency in which remuneration will be paid, and additional remuneration and/or benefits provided while working overseas and any terms and conditions of employment relating to the employee's return to the United Kingdom;

- any disciplinary rules and grievance procedures applying to the employee (or reference to documents where such details may be found). This only applies to the employer who employs over 20 employees;

- the persons to whom the employee can apply for redress of any grievances or dissatisfaction with a disciplinary decision (or reference to documents where such details may be found).

Figure 4. Statement of terms and conditions of employment (continued)

It is quite usual for the particulars which constitute the written statement of terms and conditions to be incorporated into the contract of employment, because a separate document does not then have to be issued to the employee. The model contract of employment at the end of this chapter incorporates all the particulars that must be included in the principal statement.

An employee employed for more than 13 weeks may raise a complaint with an employment tribunal if his or her employer fails to provide the written statement of the terms of employment. If a statement has been given but a question arises about particulars that should have been included in it, either employee or employer may apply to an employment tribunal.

17. **Sunday shop working**

A person employed as a shop worker, except those employed to work only on Sunday, has the following rights:

- the right not to be dismissed for refusing to work on Sundays;

- the right not to be selected for redundancy for refusing to work on Sundays;

- the right not to suffer any other detriment for refusing to work on Sundays.

There are provisions in the Sunday Trading Act 1994 entitling shop workers to opt out of and in to Sunday shop work. All shop workers who were employed on or before 26 August 1994, even those who had previously agreed to a contract requiring them to work on Sunday, and any shop workers recruited after that date whose contract of employment does not require Sunday working, but whose employer asks them to work on Sundays simply need to tell their employer that they do not wish to work on Sundays. Shop workers who entered into a contract requiring Sunday working after 26 August 1994 who agreed to do shop work on Sundays can opt out of Sunday working at any time, but they need to give their employer a written notice and then serve a three-month notice period; during the three-month notice period they will still be obliged to do the Sunday if their contract provides for it, if their employer wants them to do it; the right not to work on Sundays applies as from the end of the three-month period.

Employers are required to give every shop worker who enters into a contractual agreement to work on Sundays a written explanatory statement setting out their right to opt out. If an employer does not issue this statement within two months of the worker entering into such contract arrangement, the opt-out notice is period is reduced from 3 months to 1 month. The prescribed text of such an explanatory statement is set out in Figure 5 below.

Prescribed explanatory statement setting out statutory rights in relation to Sunday shop work

You have become employed as a shop worker and are, or can be, required under your contact of employment to do the Sunday work your contract provides for.

However, if you wish you can give a notice, as described in the next paragraph, to your employer and you will then have the right not to work in or about a shop on any Sunday on which the shop is open, once three months have passed from the date on which you give the notice.

Your notice must –

- be in writing;
- be signed and dated by you;
- say that you object to Sunday working.

For three months after you give the notice, your employer can still require you to do all the Sunday work your contract provides for. After the three-month period has ended, you have the right to complain to an employment tribunal if, because of your refusal to do Sunday work, your employer –

- dismisses you; or
- does something else detrimental to you, for example failing to promote you.

Once you have the rights described, you can surrender them only by giving your employer a further notice, signed and dated by you, saying that you wish to work on a Sunday or that you do not object Sunday working and then agreeing with your employer to work on Sundays or on a particular Sunday.

Figure 5. Prescribed explanatory statement setting out statutory rights in relation to Sunday shop work

18. **Access to Stakeholder Pensions**

An employer of more than five full-time employees (including directors) is required to offer its employees access to Stakeholder Pensions, unless they already provide a pension scheme that meets certain criteria. Stakeholder Pensions are flexible, low cost and tax-efficient retirement saving plans aimed at people earning between £9,500 and £21,600 a year who are not members of a company pension scheme. Stakeholder Pensions will not be compulsory for the employee.

It is beyond the scope of this book to cover fully the area of pensions law, but for further advice on the implementation and administration of Stakeholder Pensions contact the DSS Helpline on 0845 6012923.

19. **Data protection**

Employees have certain rights to obtain access to data which concerns them. Furthermore, employers have certain duties to comply with what is effectively a Code of Practice for the treatment of personal data. There have been a number of developments in this area, as contained in the Data Protection Act 1998; this is currently being implemented, as a result of which some of the its provisions will not be in force for some time.

It is beyond the scope of this Guide to cover this area of employment law. However, employers are advised to seek further advice from the Data Protection Registrar, details of which are set out in the Appendix.

Types of contract of employment

There is a number of different types of contract of employment. When deciding which is the most appropriate, the employer should consider the type of work, the duration of the employment and the nature of the employment relationship that is sought by both parties. Below are some of the main types of contract of employment.

Contract for an indefinite period

The majority of contracts of employment are for an indefinite period, as is the model contract included in this Guide (see page 53). They can be terminated by either party giving notice. The period of notice should be specified in the contract, but if not there is an implied term (see page 43) that the contract may be terminated upon reasonable notice. In deciding what is reasonable, the following should be taken into account:

- seniority of the employee;

- remuneration of the employee;

- age of the employee;

- length of service of the employee;

- what is usual in the trade.

However, it is more advisable to express the notice period. To determine this employers should consider:

- How long is it likely to take to find a replacement for the employee if he or she resigns?

- Will a replacement need to be trained?

- How much would it cost to make a payment in lieu of notice? Long notice periods can be very costly.

- Is it possible that the employee will work for or become a competitor? In these circumstances a relatively long notice period is advisable.

- What is reasonable to expect from the employee?

- What is competitive in the market place?

The contractual notice period must not be less than the statutory minimum period of notice referred to on page 27, but if contractual notice is longer then the longer period must be given.

Fixed-term contracts

A fixed-term contract is one that has a termination date. The duration of the fixed-term contract may be for any period. Fixed-term contracts may provide that notice to terminate can be given before the termination date. If there is no notice provision, employment is guaranteed for the full period.

A fixed-term contract will automatically expire at the end of its term. Failure to renew a fixed-term contract upon termination may lead to a valid claim for unfair dismissal or redundancy pay (see page 127). However, statutory redundancy payment rights may currently be excluded in a contract for a fixed-term of two years or more, but the right to have such an exclusion will be prohibited from October 2002.

Employers should be careful where fixed-term contracts are extended or renewed continually over long periods, and where they contain waiver clauses purporting to exclude the right to claim unfair dismissal and redundancy pay. There is some uncertainty as to whether a waiver clause remains valid where an initial fixed-term contract of the requisite length (stated above) is extended for a shorter fixed term. The crucial distinction is between an extension or renewal of a contract on substantially the same terms, and re-engagement under a new fixed-term contract. In the first case the fixed term runs from the start of the original contract until the expiry of the extension, and any waiver clause will be valid. In the second case, there is a new fixed-term contract which must be for a term of at least two years in the case or redundancy rights if any waiver clause is to be effective.

There is a potential discrimination law effect from the use of fixed-term contracts. Adverse treatment of a worker being offered a fixed-term contract rather than a permanent contract by their being less favourably treated in promotion, selection for redundancy, etc., could amount to indirect sex discrimination under the Sex Discrimination Act (see chapter 4) if the proportion of fixed-term workers is gender imbalanced and the treatment cannot be justified.

In addition, Regulations are due to come into force in October 2002 implementing European legislation on fixed-term work. The Regulations will make it unlawful to treat fixed-term employees less favourably than comparable permanent employees (unless there is an objective reason to justify the less favourable treatment). The Regulations will also limit the use of successive fixed-term contracts to employ the same person to four years.

Contracts for specific tasks

Contracts for the completion of a specific task automatically terminate once the task is completed. From October 2000, employees on such task contracts will also be protected if given less favourable treatment than comparable permanent employees.

Short-term contracts

These can be used where the work to be done can be completed within a short period of time. Where the contract is for less than three months the employee is not entitled to statutory sick pay or medical suspension pay. However, if a second such contract is entered into with the same employer and it is continuous with the first then the employer becomes liable to pay statutory sick pay or medical suspension pay.

Service contracts

This is the name given to a contract of employment for more senior employees. Service contracts may be fixed-term contracts renewable on a regular basis or they may be 'rolling' service contracts, in which the contract continues after the expiry of a fixed period and then can only be terminated by not less than, say, one year's notice.

Although service contracts can be expensive for a company they offer a measure of security and so are attractive for employees.

Directors may not have service contracts for more than five years without the agreement of the shareholders of the company at a general meeting.

Part-time contracts

An increasing number of employees is now engaged on a part-time basis. Such employees have the right not to be treated less favourably by their employers than a full-time co- worker with broadly similar qualifications, skills and experience, who is engaged in the same or broadly similar work.

Part-time workers may complain to an employment tribunal about any objectively unjustifiable less favourable treatment accorded to them by their employer and compared to that accorded to a relevant full-time worker on the ground of their part-time status. Note that workers, a broader category than employees, are protected by these rights. Broadly, in order to comply with the obligations towards the part-time worker, unless the employer has an objective justification to do otherwise, it should ensure the following:

- part-time employees should receive the same hourly rate as comparable full-time employees;

- part-time employees should receive hourly rates of overtime comparable full-time rates, once they have worked more than the normal full-time hours;

- part-time employees should not be treated less favourably than full-time employees in terms of: the rate on any contractual sick or maternity pay; the length of service required to qualify for payment; and the length of time the payment is received;

- employers must not discriminate between full-time and part-time employees over access to pensions schemes; calculation of benefits from the pension scheme for part-time staff should be on a pro rata basis as the calculation for full-time employees;

- employees should not exclude part-time staff from training simply because they work part-time (although there is no legal obligation to plan the training to accommodate their schedules);

- the contractual holiday entitlement of part-time staff should be pro rata that of full-time employees;

- contractual maternity leave and parental leave should be available to part-time employees as well as to full-time employees;

- career break schemes should be available to part-time employees in the same way;

- the criteria used to select jobs for redundancy should be objectively justified, and part-time employees must not be less favourably treated than comparable full-time employees.

Part-time workers also have anti-victimisation rights. Any dismissal of a part-time worker because he or she has exercised any right under the Part-time Worker (Prevention of Less Favourable Treatment) Regulations 2000 is automatically unfair, regardless of the worker's length of service or whether the employee is above normal retiring age. Such workers also have the right not to suffer any detriment short of dismissal on grounds of that action.

Please note that there is currently no express statutory obligation to consider applications from people who want to work part-time or in a job share or in any other flexible way. Equally, there is no express obligation to allow an existing full-time worker to go part-time or vice versa. Employers should, however, bear in mind that inflexible working practices may be challenged as indirectly sex discriminatory. From April 2003 there will be a right to request to work flexi-time.

Terms of contract

Express and implied terms

Usually, the parties to the contract will have expressly stated the major terms of the contract. These may be written or oral but it is obviously preferable to put these terms in writing in order to minimise future disputes. The model contract at the end of this chapter is an example of standard, express, written terms in a contract of employment. Even though in practice express, oral terms may be just as binding as written ones, they are very much more difficult to prove.

In addition to the express terms of the contract, all contracts of employment have what is known as 'implied terms'.

Implied terms are not stated expressly in the contract because:

- they are too obvious to be recorded; or

- they are common practice within the particular business or industry and are precise, reasonable and well known; or

- they are necessary to make the contract work; or

- the parties to the contract have shown by their behaviour their acceptance of such terms.

A term is not implied simply because it would be reasonable to include it. There are terms which are accepted as commonly implied in employment contracts relating to the employer's and the employee's duties, as shown in Figure 6 overleaf.

Employer's duties

- to pay **wages** (see below)
- to **co-operate** with the employee and maintain mutual trust and confidence
- to take reasonable care for the **health and safety** of the employee
- to take reasonable steps to bring to the employee's attention any **contractual rights** which are dependent on them taking action, but which the employee may be reasonably unaware of
- to exercise **pension rights** in good faith
- to deal reasonably and promptly with **employees' grievances**
- to give a reasonable period of **notice of termination** when no specific period of notice has been agreed

Employee's duties

- to work for the employer with due **diligence and care**
- to **co-operate** with the employer, including obeying lawful orders and not impeding the employer's business
- to follow a duty of **fidelity** i.e. not compete with the employer and not disclose confidential information unless in the public interest
- to take reasonable care for their own **safety** and that of fellow employees
- to give a reasonable period of **notice of termination** when no specific period of notice has been agreed

Figure 6. Common implied terms

In addition to those listed in Figure 6, terms may be implied into a contract of employment by legislation, for example equality clauses which are implied by the Equal Pay Act 1970; these terms automatically apply to any contract.

Terms may also be incorporated into a contract of employment from other sources. Prime examples are terms which may be implied into an individual contract through collective agreements and work rules or Staff Handbooks.

Unenforceable terms

1. **Unlawful terms or terms contrary to public policy**

    For example, a contract which has the effect of being a fraud on the Inland Revenue or a contract under which a foreign employee works illegally without a work permit.

2. **Terms purporting to contract out of employment protection legislation**

3. **Discriminatory terms**

    For example, on the grounds of sex, race or disability.

4. **Terms in restraint of trade** if their main purpose is to restrain competition

    Such terms *are* enforceable, however, if their main purpose is to protect something in which the employer has a legitimate business interest worthy of protection. For any such clause to be enforceable it needs to be carefully drafted, taking into account the nature of the employee's work. If the clause is too wide it will be void. The courts will not rewrite clauses to make them enforceable; an example of a restraint of trade clause is given at clause 10 of the model employment contract at the end of this chapter.

5. **Terms which purport to exclude or restrict liability for death or personal injury resulting from negligence**

    In the case of loss or damage other than death or personal injury a contract term may only exclude or restrict liability for negligence if it satisfies the requirement of reasonableness (for further details on this see the Unfair Contract Terms Act 1977).

Variation of contract

An employer does not have an automatic right to vary an employee's terms of employment. The extent to which employers can unilaterally change an employee's terms or working arrangements will depend entirely on the terms themselves.

Existing terms

Flexibility may be expressly built into the contract by, for example, the inclusion of wide terms or narrow, but changeable terms. An example of the former is 'You may be required to work anywhere in the UK' while an example of the latter is 'You will work 8 hours in 24, day, night or shift work'. Another way flexibility may have been built into the contract is by the use of terms which can be altered in content or removed. For example, entitlement to a bonus may be stated to be at the manager's discretion and/or the employer may reserve the right to remove entitlement to a bonus without compensation.

The contract may also contain what is known as 'machinery for change'. For example, the Staff Handbook 'as issued from time to time' may be stated to be incorporated. This would mean that matters dealt with in the handbook could be changed and the change incorporated into the contract, without the need of the employee's express consent.

If the contract contains such flexible clauses or incorporates machinery for change then the employer will be able to alter the terms in line with these clauses provided the implementation of such alterations is carried out in a reasonable manner, e.g. if a mobility clause is included in the contract, the employer should give reasonable notice before requiring an employee to relocate.

If there is no flexibility or machinery for change then employers must follow the correct procedure if they want to alter an employee's terms of employment, in order to minimise the possibility of claims for damages and/or compensation relating to the change.

Offering new terms to the employee

The first step for the employer is to offer the new terms to the employee. He can either accept or reject them. Acceptance must be positive, unequivocal and unconditional. There is no particular form of offering or acceptance required, so it can be oral, written or by conduct. Letter 8 at the end of this chapter provides an example of an employer altering the terms of an employee's employment. However, by doing nothing an employee cannot be said to have accepted the new terms. The only time doing nothing can amount to acceptance is when the contract contains a term making this so. An example of such a term would be, 'If you do not object in writing within 14 days you will be deemed to have accepted the change'. It is possible for an employee to accept the new terms by his conduct: if he changes his behaviour to comply with a term in the offer (for example he turns up for work at a new time) he will be taken to have accepted the new terms.

Dismiss and offer employment on new terms

If the employee does not accept the changes the only other option for the employer is to dismiss him and offer employment on the new terms. However, by doing this the employer may become liable for claims for breach of contract, unfair dismissal or redundancy if the correct procedures are not followed and the appropriate reasons for dismissal do not exist. Termination of employment is dealt with in greater detail in chapter 5 but if employers wish to take this route it is suggested that they take advice before doing so.

Staff Handbook

An employer will always have a number of practices and procedures that it will want to apply to its employees. Generally it is advisable for these to be contained in one document, which should be issued to all employees at the commencement of their employment. Employees should be asked to confirm that they have read and understood the Staff Handbook.

However, it is also important for the employer to retain the ability to amend the practices and procedures in the Staff Handbook, and therefore it should be stated that the Staff Handbook, as amended from time to time, applies to all employees at the introduction of the Staff Handbook. The Staff Handbook should also be referred to in the contract (see clause 15 of the model employment contract at page 56).

The Staff Handbook may contain a variety of procedures and will vary from employer, but in nearly all cases it should include the following:

- Equal Opportunities Policy
- Disciplinary Rules & Procedures
- Grievance Procedure

• Health & Safety Policy

A model Staff Handbook is shown on page 59 which includes examples of matters that an employer may wish to include in a Staff Handbook and may be adapted according to the employer's needs and requirements. It is beyond the scope of this book to cover all administrative issues that may need to be included in a Staff Handbook, so it is important that an employer considers its own needs and requirements when preparing its own Staff Handbook.

Use of telephones, email and the internet

Because of the way in which people work has changed, with the growth of email, voicemail and other office-based communications, there has been an increase in an employer's need to monitor such communications. It is essential for an employer to be clear with the employees the extent to which it will tolerate the use of these business tools for personal use. Not only does this reduce the likelihood of employees overusing the telephones, email and the internet and spending less time carrying out their duties, but also if they do abuse the system, the employer is in a stronger position to take disciplinary action because they can point to a clear procedure which has been violated.

There is a variety of reasons why an employer may wish to have the right to monitor email or telephone calls, such as a need to open the email of an employee who is on holiday, the need to monitor performance or unauthorised use or in particular, use of offence material or detection of damaging computer viruses.

DEFINITION

Recent law entitles employers to intercept certain types of communications in defined circumstances, without the consent of the sender or the recipient, where the interception is only for the purpose of monitoring or keeping a record of communications relevant to the business in question. The defined circumstances where such interception is authorised are:

• to establish the existence of facts relevant to the business (e.g. where it may be necessary to know specific facts of a conversation);

• to check the company is complying with external regulatory or internal regulatory rules or guidelines;

- to ascertain or demonstrate standards which are or ought to be achieved by persons using the system (e.g. for the purposes of staff training or quality control);

- to prevent or detect crime (e.g. to detect fraud);

- to investigate or detect the unauthorised use of telecommunications systems (e.g. to ensure employees do not breach company rules or policies on the use of the email system or internet);

- to ensure the effective operation of the system (e.g. monitoring for viruses).

An employer is also entitled to monitor, *but not record without consent*, for the following purposes:

- For determining whether or not the communications are relevant to the business (e.g. where a member of staff is on holiday or off sick, it may be necessary to access their emails to determine whether they are relevant to the business).

- For monitoring communications to confidential, anonymous, counselling or support helplines. This includes monitoring of calls to confidential helplines to protect or support helpline staff.

Whilst this law authorises the monitoring or recording of a wide range of communications, such information is likely to be covered by the data protection principles contained in the Data Protection Act 1998 and therefore must be processed in a way that does not violate those principles. The Data Protection Commissioner has issued a code of practice that deals with the question of email and telephone monitoring. Broadly, employers must only monitor after first establishing that there is a problem that calls for monitoring. In respect of email, the employer should carry out traffic monitoring to determine whether the system is being abused and in relation to telephone monitoring an itemised call record may be an appropriate initial step. The code makes it clear that there should only be monitoring where there is a real business need and the methods used to carry it out should be proportionate and not unduly intrusive into the individual's privacy. Accordingly, employers should be very careful in exercising their right to monitor under this new legislation.

Employees and the self-employed

This chapter has so far dealt with the employment relationship i.e. between an employer and employee. However, any person who works for another person or organisation in return for remuneration has a contractual relationship with them or it, but it may be as a consultant or self-employed person. There is an extremely important distinction between an employee and a self-employed person, because their legal rights differ in a number of ways.

DEFINITION

A *contract of employment* (sometimes referred to as a *contract of service*) is the name given to the agreement an employee has with an employer. A *contract for services* is the name given to the agreement between a self-employed person (or independent sub-contractor) and the person or organisation to whom he or she is providing the services.

To distinguish between a contract of employment and a contract for services it is necessary to look at the reality of the relationship, not merely the name of the agreement.

How to distinguish a contract of employment from a contract for services

Questions to consider in determining whether a person is an employee or is self-employed are:

1. Are there mutual obligations on the employer to provide work for the person engaged and on the person engaged to perform work for the employer?

2. Is he performing services for other people as a person in business on his own account?

3. Is he working under the orders of the person to whom he is supplying the services who controls when, how and what he must do?

4. Does he provide his own machinery and equipment?

5. Does he hire his own helpers?

6. Does he take a degree of financial risk?

7.   Is the engagement for a specific, finite project or does it carry a degree of responsibility for ongoing administration or management?

8.   Does he have the possibility of profiting from sound management in the performance of his tasks?

The greater degree of personal responsibility the person engaged undertakes in any of the above, the more likely he is to be considered self-employed rather than an employee. Other factors may include the method of payment, the method of paying tax and national insurance, payment during absence for illness or for holidays, membership of company pension schemes and a prohibition on working for other companies or individuals.

Although the above questions are relevant considerations, they will not be appropriate in every case and the answer to the question is not found by merely using these questions as a check list. It is important to assess each case individually.

If there is any doubt as to the nature of the relationship the parties may agree on what the legal situation between them is to be. However, it will not be conclusive when questions of tax, social security or statutory employment protection arise. If the matter goes to a court or tribunal all the circumstances will be considered to ascertain the true nature of the relationship.

To add to the confusion, some of the more recent legislation (such as the Working Time Regulations) replaces the term 'employee' with the term 'worker'. A worker includes both employees and others who provide services personally (although not under a client relationship), but does not include a person who is genuinely self-employed. This greatly increases the number of people protected by such legislation.

Practical and legal implications

Employees' statutory rights are dealt with separately in this chapter. The self-employed do not have these statutory rights but here is a list of the rights and obligations they do have:

Rights of the self-employed

- equal opportunities, i.e. non-discrimination on the grounds of race, sex or disability

- to be provided with a safe place of work and system of work

- to be paid wages or fees free of any deductions not properly authorised.

Obligations of self-employed

- to work with due skill and diligence

- to pay income tax under Schedule D

- to pay self-employed person's National Insurance contributions

- to fulfil contractual obligations

The Inland Revenue has introduced rules to remove opportunities for the avoidance of tax and Class One National Insurance Contributions by the use of intermediaries, such as service companies or partnerships, in circumstances where the individual worker would otherwise be considered to be an employee. The new rules determine that, where workers meet the definition of employees in relation to work done for their clients, they will pay broadly the same tax and National Insurance Contributions as an employee, even if they provide their services through an intermediary. For further details, please see the Inland Revenue website at www.inlandrevenue.gov.uk.

Model employment contract

1 This must be no later than
two months after the
employment commences.
Any changes must be
notified to the employee
within one month of the
change. No statement is
required to be given to an
employee employed under a
contract for less than one
month.

2 For agreements entered
into prior to 22 August 1996
the Employment Protection
(Consolidation) Act 1978
applies.

3 If employment with a
previous employer is to be
counted as a period of
continuous employment
this, and the date it began,
must be stated.

<u>EMPLOYMENT CONTRACT</u>

THIS AGREEMENT IS MADE the *20th day of August 2002*.[1]

BETWEEN (1) *Ace Fabrics Limited of Unit 2, Boxwood Trading Estate, Kings Langley HO3 2HT* (the "Employer") and (2) *Susan Porter of 12 Elm Drive, Milton Keynes ME9 427* (the "Employee")

This document sets out the terms and conditions of employment which are required to be given to the Employee under Section 1 Employment Rights Act 1996[2] and which apply at the date hereof.

1. COMMENCEMENT AND JOB TITLE

The Employer agrees to employ the Employee from *2nd September 2002* in the capacity of *Machinist* at *Unit 2, Boxwood Trading Estate*. No employment with a previous employer will be counted as part of the Employee's period of continuous employment[3]. The Employee's duties which this job entails are set out in the job description attached to this statement. The job description may from time to time be reasonably modified as necessary to meet the needs of the Employer's business.

2. SALARY

The Employer shall pay the Employee a salary of *£13,500* per year payable by credit transfer at monthly intervals on the last day of each month. The Company shall review the Employee's salary at such intervals as it shall at its sole discretion decide.

3. DEDUCTIONS

The Employer shall be entitled at any time during the employment and in any event on termination, howsoever arising, to deduct from the Employee's salary hereunder any monies due from him or owed from him to the company.

4. HOURS OF EMPLOYMENT

The Employee's normal hours of employment shall be *9.00 am* to *5.00 pm* on *Mondays* to *Fridays* during which time the Employee may take up to one hour for lunch between the hours of *12.00 pm and 2.00 pm*, and the Employee may from time to time be required to work such additional hours as is reasonable to meet the requirements of the Employer's business at an overtime rate of *£7.50* per hour.

4 If the employer does not wish to pay normal remuneration during sickness they should state that the statutory sick pay rules apply.

5 Where a collective agreement directly affects the terms and conditions of employment the following should be inserted as clause 6:'The terms of the collective agreement dated [ ] made between [ ] and [ ] shall deemed to be included in this agreement'.

Model employment contract (continued)

5. HOLIDAYS

The Employee shall be entitled to *20* days' holiday per calendar year at full pay in addition to the normal public holidays. Holidays must be taken at times convenient to the Employer and sufficient notice of intention to take holiday must be given to the Employee's supervisor. No more than 2 weeks' holiday must be taken at any one time unless permission is given by *the Employee's* supervisor. Holiday untaken in the calendar year to which it relates will be lost and may not be carried forward.

The Employee shall be entitled to payment in lieu of holiday accrued due but untaken at the date of termination of his or her employment. If at the date of termination the Employee has taken holiday in excess of his or her accrued entitlement a corresponding deduction will be made from his or her final payment.

6. SICKNESS

6.1 If the Employee is absent from work on account of sickness or injury, he or she or someone on his or her behalf should inform the Employer of the reason for the absence as soon as possible but no later than *12.00 pm* on the working day on which absence first occurs.

6.2 *The Company reserves the right to ask the Employee at any stage of absence to produce a medical certificate and/or to undergo a medical examination.*

6.3 The Employee shall be paid normal remuneration during sickness absence for a maximum of *4 weeks* in any period of *12 months* provided that the Employee provides the Employer with a medical certificate in the case of absence of more than *7 consecutive days*. Such remuneration will be less the amount of any Statutory Sick Pay or Social Security sickness benefits to which the Employee may be entitled. Entitlement to payment is subject to notification of absence and production of medical certificates as required above.[4]

7. COLLECTIVE AGREEMENTS

There are no collective agreements in force directly relating to the terms of your employment.[5]

6 Where no pension scheme exists this must be stated and where no contracting out certificate is in force this must also be stated. However, please note the requirements to provide access to stakeholder pensions from 8 October 2001 (page 38).

7 These are minimum periods required by law but they may be increased by agreement.

Model employment contract (continued)

8.   PENSION

The Employee shall be entitled to join the Employer's pension scheme, the details of which are set out in the Employer's booklet/leaflet which is entitled *Your Pension at Ace Fabrics* and which is available on request. A contracting-out certificate under the Pension Schemes Act 1993 is in force in respect of this employment.[6]

9.   TERMINATION

The Employer may terminate this Agreement by giving written notice to the Employee as follows:

(a)   With not less than one week's notice during the first two years of continuous employment; then

(b)   With not less than a further one week's notice for each full year of continuous employment after the first two years until the 12th year of continuous employment; and

(c)   With not less than 12 weeks' notice after 12 years of continuous employment.[7]

The Employer may terminate this Agreement without notice or payment in lieu of notice in the case of serious or persistent misconduct such as to cause a major breach of the Employer's disciplinary rules.

The Employee may terminate this Agreement by one week's written notice to the Employer.

After notice of termination has been given by either party, provided the Employee continues to be paid and to enjoy his or her full contractual benefits under the terms of this Agreement, the Employer may in its absolute discretion for all or part of the notice period exclude the Employee from the premises of the Employer and require that he or she carries out duties other than those specified in his or her job description or require that he or she carries out no duties at all until the termination of his or her employment.

10.   CONFIDENTIALITY

The Employee is aware that during his or her employment he or she may be party to confidential information concerning the Employer and the Employer's business. The Employee shall not during the term of his or her employment disclose or allow the disclosure of any confidential information (except in the proper course of his or her employment) other than

8 The employer may choose any number of months or years that are necessary to protect its business interests in relation to the employee in question and in any event, even for the most senior employee any more than two years is likely to render this clause unenforceable at law. Also see note on terms in restraint of trade on page 45.

9 It is sometimes recommended that the customers or clients are named either in the contract or a separate schedule (which may be updated on an annual basis) to ensure better certainty in this clause.

10 This period should be between one and three years if it is to remain enforceable by the employer.

11 See model procedures that follow.

Model employment contract (continued)

information which has come into the public domain or information that the Employee is entitled to disclose under the Public Interest Disclosure Act 1998.

After the termination of this Agreement the Employee shall not disclose or use any of the Employer's trade secrets or any other information which is of a sufficiently high degree of confidentiality to amount to a trade secret. The Employer shall be entitled to apply for an injunction to prevent such disclosure or use and to seek any other remedy including without limitation the recovery of damages in the case of such disclosure or use.

11. NON-SOLICITATION

For a period of *six months*[8] after the termination of this Agreement the Employee shall not solicit or seek business from any customers or clients of the Employer who were customers or clients[9] of the Employer at the time during the *12 months*[10] immediately preceding the termination of this Agreement.

12. DISCIPLINE AND GRIEVANCE

The Employer's disciplinary rules and procedure and the grievance and appeal procedure in connection with these rules are set out in the Employer's leaflets entitled *Disciplinary Rules and Procedure at Ace Fabrics Limited* and *Grievance Procedure at Ace Fabrics Limited* respectively which are attached hereto.[11]

13. NOTICES

All communications including notices required to be given under this Agreement shall be in writing and shall be sent either by personal service or first class post to the parties' respective addresses.

14. SEVERABILITY

If any provision of this Agreement should be held to be invalid it shall to that extent be severed and the remaining provisions shall continue to have full force and effect.

15. STAFF HANDBOOK

Further details of the arrangements affecting your employment are published in the *Staff Handbook* as issued from time to time. These are largely of an administrative nature but, so far as relevant, are to be treated as incorporated in this Agreement.

12 Only such information as is presently held by the Employer, or may be held by the Employer in the future should be included in the list, as the wider the clause is, the less likely employees will agree to it.

13 If the data are going to be transferred outside the UK, specific consents need to be obtained.

Model employment contract (continued)

16. GOVERNING LAW

This Agreement shall be construed in accordance with the laws of England and Wales and shall be subject to the exclusive jurisdiction of the English Courts.

Please acknowledge receipt of this statement and your agreement to the terms set out in it by signing the attached copy of this letter and returning it to *Mr Smith*.

17. MISCELLANEOUS

A person who is not a party to this Agreement shall not have any rights under the Contracts (Rights of Third Parties) Act 1999 to enforce any term of this Agreement.

18. DATA PROTECTION

During the course of recruitment and thereafter, the Employer will, for reasons related to your employment, process data relating to you, and will do so in accordance with statutory principles governing fair and lawful processing. You specifically consent to the fair and lawful processing of information defined as personal sensitive data.

For the purposes of this paragraph 'personal sensitive data' shall mean information concerning[12]:

- your racial or ethnic origin;
- your political opinions;
- your religious beliefs or beliefs of a similar nature;
- your membership or non-membership of a Trade Union;
- your physical or mental health or condition;
- your sex life;
- any commission or alleged commission by you of any offence; or
- any proceedings for any offence committed or alleged to have been committed by you, the disposal of such proceedings or the sentence of any court of such proceedings.

For the purposes of this paragraph 'processing' includes the obtaining, recording or holding of information or data or carrying out any operation or set of operations on the information or data, including organising, altering, retrieving, consulting, using, disclosing, combining or destroying the information or data[13].

Model employment contract (continued)

IN WITNESS OF WHICH the parties hereto have signed this Agreement the day and year first above written.

SIGNED _____   _____

Signed by or on behalf of
Ace Fabrics Ltd   in the presence of (witness)

_____   Name _____

_____   Address _____

_____   _____

DATED   Occupation

_____   _____

SIGNED _____   _____

Signed by the Employee   in the presence of (witness)

_____   Name _____

_____   Address _____

_____   _____

DATED   Occupation

_____   _____

Model Staff Handbook

STAFF HANDBOOK[1]

Table of contents

1. Introduction
2. Equal Opportunities Policy
3. Health & Safety Policy
4. Training
5. Business expenses
6. Attendance and timekeeping
7. Appearance
8. Alcohol
9. Smoking
10. Use email and the internet
11. Use of telephones and other facilities
12. Acceptance of gifts
13. Data Protection Policy
14. Whistleblowing Policy
15. Disciplinary Rules and Procedure
16. Grievance Policy

1. Introduction

This Staff Handbook provides you with a summary of the policies and procedures that operate in the Company. It should be read in conjunction with your contract of employment as both documents form part of your terms and conditions of employment.

To respond to the changing needs of the Company as well as changes in legislation, the policies and procedures may need to be amended from time to time and when this occurs you will be informed of these changes.

If you have any questions about this Staff Handbook please contact your manager.

2. Equal Opportunities Policy

The Company's aim is to ensure that all of its employees and job applicants are treated equally irrespective of disability, race, colour, religion, nationality, ethnic origin, age, sex, sexual orientation or marital status. The Company shall appoint, train, develop and promote on the basis of merit and ability.

2 Where employers consider a more detailed policy which incorporates a harassment and bullying policy is more appropriate they should seek guidance from the EOC, CRE or ACAS.

3 Specific rules relating to the health and safety rules particular to the organisation need to be added here.

Model Staff Handbook (continued)

All employees have a duty both morally and legally not to discriminate against individuals. This means that there shall be no discrimination on account of disability, race, colour, religion, nationality, ethnic origin, age, sex, sexual orientation or marital status. Employees have personal responsibility for the practical application of the Company's Equal Opportunities Policy which extends to the treatment of members of the public and employees.

Managers and supervisors who are involved in the recruitment, selection, promotion and training of employees have special responsibility for the practical application of the Company's Equal Opportunities Policy.

The grievance procedure is available to any employee who believes that he or she may have been unfairly discriminated against.

Disciplinary action under the disciplinary procedure shall be taken against any employee who is found to have committed an act of unlawful discrimination. Discriminatory conduct and sexual or racial harassment shall be regarded as gross misconduct.

If there is any doubt about appropriate treatment under the Company's Equal Opportunities Policy, employees should consult their manager.[2]

3. Health & Safety Policy

The Company recognises that it is responsible for ensuring so far as is reasonably practicable the health & safety welfare at work for its employees. The Company believes that pro-active management health and safety issues are an integral part of its obligations to its employees and to the wider community. This policy statement sets out in broad terms the legal responsibilities owed by the Company and by employees in relation to health and safety issues. It will only be possible for the Company to comply with these legal obligations if both its employees and any self-employed third parties on the Company's premises understands that they are under a duty to take reasonable care for the health and safety of themselves and any of their colleagues who may be affected by their acts or omissions and that they are required to cooperate with the Company to enable the Company to perform its obligations.[3]

4. Training

The Company is committed to the continuous development of all its employees. It is vital that employees possess the skills and knowledge to enable them to perform their duties effectively. Any needs should be discussed with the employee's manager on an annual basis. The Company may in its absolute discretion provide financial assistance for external training courses which have relevance to the employees' current or likely future duties with the Company.

5. Business expenses

Employees will be reimbursed for fair and reasonable expenses that are incurred while conducting business on behalf of the Company. Such reimbursement will be made by the

Model Staff Handbook (continued)

Company upon submission of an expense report approved by the employees' manager. Abuse of this right to claim expenses is considered to be gross misconduct which may result in dismissal.

6. Attendance and timekeeping

Employees are expected to attend work punctually at the hours defined in their contract of employment. Employees must receive prior approval from their manager to leave the Company premises during working hours except during lunchbreaks. This will enable the Company to ensure that employees can be located in the event of an emergency.

7. Appearance

Employees are expected to maintain a standard of personal hygiene, appearance and dress appropriate to their job responsibilities.

8. Alcohol

The consumption of alcohol is not allowed on Company premises at any time except where authorised by the employees' manager. No employee should report to work whilst under the influence of alcohol. Breach of this policy may amount to gross misconduct which may result in dismissal.

9. Smoking

Smoking on Company premises is prohibited, apart from designated areas. Employees who do not comply with the no smoking policy, will be subject to disciplinary action.

10. Use of email and the internet

Employees are encouraged to use email and the internet at work as a fast and reliable method of communication with significant advantages for business. However, employees need to be careful not to expose both themselves and the Company to certain risks and offences and that the misuse of these facilities can cause.

Use of external and internal email

- Employees must word all emails appropriately in the same professional manner as if they were composing a letter.

- The content of any email message sent must be neither defamatory, abusive nor illegal and must accord with the Company's Equal Opportunities Policy. Sending and receiving of obscene or pornographic or other offensive material is not only considered to be gross misconduct but may also constitute a criminal offence.

Model Staff Handbook (continued)

- Employees must be careful of what is said in email messages as the content could give rise to both personal liability or create liability for the Company. Employees must also avoid entering into commitments of themselves or on behalf of the Company over the internet without having received prior and express authorisation to do so or unless this forms part of their normal day-to-day activities and has been so authorised by the Company.

- The Company reserves the right to monitor the content of emails sent and received and may undertake monitoring of both the content and extent of use of emails. Employees wishing to send confidential non-work related emails should do so on their own equipment in their own time at their own home and should tell personal email contacts never to send any personal emails to them at work.

- Employees must ensure that they have the correct email address for the intended recipients. If employees inadvertently misdirect an email they should contact their manager immediately on becoming aware of their mistake. Failure to do so may lead to disciplinary action being taken against them.

- Employees must not send any information that the Company considers to be confidential or sensitive over the email. The Company, in particular considers the following information inappropriate for transmission over email: [*provide list of confidential/sensitive information*].

- The email facility is provided for business purposes only. Employees must limit personal usage to a minimum and must abide by the above guidelines concerning the content of emails. Excessive personal usage or abuse of the guidelines concerning the content of emails may lead to the withdrawal of email and internet access and/or disciplinary action which could result in dismissal.

- Employees should at all times remember that email messages may have to be disclosed as evidence at any Court proceedings or investigations by regulatory bodies and therefore may be prejudicial to both their or the Company's interests. Employees should consider that hard copies of emails may be taken and backup discs may retain records of emails even when these have been deleted from the system.

- Disciplinary action under the disciplinary procedure shall be taken against any employee who is found to be in breach of these guidelines and depending upon the circumstances and seriousness of the breach, this may result in summary dismissal.

Using the internet

- Employees must not use the internet to gain unauthorised access or attempt to gain unauthorised access to computer material or private databases.

- Employees must not use the internet for personal purposes whether during work hours or otherwise as this puts an unnecessary strain upon the Company's computer network. Internet access is available purely for business use and it should be used for work related purposes only.

- Internet access may be monitored by the Company and the Company will conduct an audit of internet usage from time to time. Should any breach of these internet guide-

Model Staff Handbook (continued)

lines be discovered then employees may, in addition to having internet access being withdrawn, be the subject of disciplinary action which, in the case of serious breach, may result in dismissal.

- Employees may not subscribe to any news list or groups or commit themselves to receiving information from any group or body without first informing their manager. Employees are requested not to view sites which require the downloading of software from the internet even where this would be free of charge without the prior approval of their manager. Staff are reminded of the risk of computer virus.

- Employees must not attempt to download or retrieve illegal, pornographic, liable, sexist, racist, offensive or unlawful material. Attempts to access such material will constitute a disciplinary offence and, in addition to access to the internet being withdrawn, the member of staff may be subject to disciplinary action which may result in dismissal.

- Information on the internet may not have been placed there with the owner's permission. Therefore employees must obtain the permission of the copyright owner before transmitting, copying or downloading such information. Where the copyright owner's consent has clearly been given employees must comply with any terms and conditions stipulated concerning the downloading of such information.

- Information may contain viruses and therefore should not be downloaded from the internet without first obtaining the approval of *Mr. Smith* and/or instructions of *Mr. Smith* concerning the downloading of such information which must be followed. Employees should only download such information that is required for a business purpose. The downloading of information of whatever nature for personal purposes is not permitted.

11. Use of telephones and other facilities

The Company's telephones, mail, faxes and photocopying facilities are provided for business purposes only. Employees must limit personal usage to a minimum. Excessive personal usage may lead to the withdrawal of email and internet access and/or disciplinary action which could result in dismissal.

12. Acceptance of gifts

Employees must not accept directly or indirectly any payment or any other benefit or thing of value of more than nominal value from any supply or customer or from anyone else with any actual or perspective business relationship with the company.

Friendships may develop between customers and employees. However, any relationship between a customer and an employee which is likely to jeopardise business relations in the company is not acceptable. Employees must use their common sense to avoid any actual relationships.

Model Staff Handbook (continued)

13. Data Protection Policy

Employees may be required to give certain information relating to themselves in order that the Company may properly carry out its duties, rights and obligations as the employer. The Company will process and control such data principally for personnel, administrative and payroll purposes.

The term 'processing' may include the Company obtaining, recording or holding the information or data or carrying out any set of operation or operations on the information or data, including organising, altering, retrieving, consulting, using, disclosing, or destroying the information or data. The Company will adopt appropriate technical and organisational measures to prevent the unauthorised or unlawful processing or disclosure of data.

[It may be necessary to transfer data relating to employees outside of the UK in order that the Company may properly carry out its duties, rights and obligation, in the following circumstances and to the following countries: *France, USA etc.*]

Employees are requested to sign the attached consent form giving consent to the Company to process data relating to them which may include sensitive data.[4]

14. Whistleblowing Policy

Employees may, in properly carrying out their duties, have access to, or come into contact with information of a confidential nature. Their terms and conditions provide that except in the proper performance of their duties, employees are forbidden from disclosing or making use of in any form whatsoever such confidential information. However, the law allows employees to make a 'protected disclosure' of certain information. In order to be 'protected' a disclosure must relate to a specific subject matter (listed below) and the disclosure must also be made in an appropriate way.

If in the course of employment, an employee becomes aware of information which they reasonably believe tends to show one or more of the following, they must use the company's disclosure procedure set out below:

- That a criminal offence has been committed, is being committed or is likely to be committed;

- That a person has failed, is failing or is likely to fail to comply with any legal obligation to which he is subject;

- That a miscarriage of justice that has occurred, is occurring, or is likely to occur;

- That the health or safety of any individual has been, is being, or is likely to be, endangered;

- That the environment, has been, is being, or is likely to be, damaged;

- That information tending to show any of the above, is being or is likely to be deliberately concealed.

Model Staff Handbook (continued)

Disclosure Procedure

Information which an employee reasonably believes tends to show one or more of the above should promptly be disclosed to their manager so that any appropriate action can be taken. If it is inappropriate to make such a disclosure to the manager the employee should speak to *Mr. Jones*.

Employees will suffer no detriment of any sort for making such a disclosure in accordance with this procedure. However, failure to follow this procedure may result in the disclosure of information losing its 'protected status'. For further guidance in relation to this matter or concerning the use of the disclosure procedure generally, employees should speak in confidence to *Mr. Jones*.

15. Disciplinary Rules and Procedure

1. The Company's aim is to encourage improvement in individual performance and conduct. Employees are required to treat members of the public and other employees equally in accordance with the Equal Opportunities Policy. This procedure sets out the action which will be taken when disciplinary rules are breached.

2. Principles:

    (i)   The list of rules is not to be regarded as an exhaustive list.

    (ii)   The procedure is designed to establish the facts quickly and to deal consistently with disciplinary issues. No disciplinary action will be taken until the matter has been fully investigated.

    (iii) At every stage employees will have the opportunity to state their case and have a right to be accompanied by a fellow employee or a trade union official of their choice at the hearings.

    (iv)   Only a Director has the right to suspend or dismiss. An employee may, however, be given a verbal or written warning by their immediate superior.

    (v)   An employee has the right to appeal against any disciplinary decision.

3. The Rules:

    Breaches of the Company's disciplinary rules which can lead to disciplinary action are:

    *   failure to observe a reasonable order or instruction;

    *   failure to observe a health and safety requirement;

    *   inadequate time keeping;

    *   absence from work without proper cause (including taking parental leave dishonestly);

    *   theft or removal of the Company's property;

    *   loss, damage to or misuse of the Company's property through negligence or carelessness;

Model Staff Handbook (continued)

- conduct detrimental to the interests of the Company;
- incapacity for work due to being under the influence of alcohol or illegal drugs;
- physical assault or gross insubordination;
- committing an act outside work or being convicted for a criminal offence which is liable adversely to affect the performance of the contract of employment and/or the relationship between the employee and the Company;
- failure to comply with the Company's Equal Opportunities Policy.

4. The Procedure:

   (i) *Oral warning*

   If conduct or performance is unsatisfactory, the employee will be given a formal oral warning, which will be recorded. The warning will be disregarded after six months' satisfactory service.

   (ii) *Written warning*

   If the offence is serious, if there is no improvement in standards, or if a further offence occurs, a written warning will be given which will include the reason for the warning and a note that, if there is no improvement after twelve months, a final written warning will be given.

   (iii) *Final written warning*

   If conduct or performance is still unsatisfactory, or if a further serious offence occurs within the 12-month period, a final written warning will be given making it clear that any recurrence of the offence or other serious misconduct within a period of one month will result in dismissal.

   (iv) *Dismissal*

   If there is no satisfactory improvement or if further serious misconduct occurs, the employee will be dismissed.

   (v) *Gross misconduct*

   If, after investigation, it is confirmed that an employee has committed an offence of the following nature (the list is not exhaustive) the normal consequence will be dismissal:

   - theft of or damage to the Company's property, incapacity for work due to being under the influence of alcohol or illegal drugs, physical assault and gross insubordination, discrimination or harassment contrary to the Company's Equal Opportunities Policy.

   While the alleged gross misconduct is being investigated the employee may be suspended, during which time he or she will be paid the normal hourly rate. Any decision to dismiss will be taken by the employer only after a full investigation.

Model Staff Handbook (continued)

(vi) *Appeals*

An employee who wishes to appeal against any disciplinary decision must do so to *Mr. Jones* within two working days. The employer will hear the appeal and decide the case as impartially as possible.

16. Grievance Procedure

1. The following procedure shall be applied to settle all disputes or grievances concerning an employee or employees of the Company (but excluding those relating to redundancy selection).

2. Principles:

    (i) It is the intention of both parties that employees should be encouraged to have direct contact with management to resolve their problems.

    (ii) The procedure for resolution of grievances and avoidance of disputes is available if the parties are unable to agree a solution to a problem.

    (iii) Should a matter be referred to this procedure for resolution, both parties should accept that it should be progressed as speedily as possible, with a joint commitment that every effort will be made to ensure that such a reference takes no longer than seven working days to complete.

    (iv) Pending resolution of the grievance, the same conditions prior to its notification shall continue to apply, except in those circumstances where such a continuation would have damaging effects upon the Company's business.

    (v) It is agreed between the parties that where the grievance is of a collective nature, i.e. affecting more than one employee, it shall be referred initially to (ii) of the procedure.

    (vi) If the employee's immediate supervisor/manager is the subject of the grievance and for this reason the employee does not wish the grievance to be heard by him or her, it shall be referred initially to (ii) of the procedure.

3. The Procedure:

    (i) Where an employee has a grievance, he shall raise the matter with his or her immediate supervisor/manager. If the grievance concerns the performance of a duty by the Company in relation to an employee, the employee shall have a right to be accompanied by a fellow worker or trade union official if they make a request to be so accompanied.

    (ii) If the matter has not been resolved at (i), it shall be referred to a more senior manager or director and the shop steward, full time trade union officer, or fellow employee, if requested shall be present. A statement summarising the main details of the grievance and the reasons for the failure to agree must be prepared and signed by both parties.

5 An employer should only include those categories that are relevant to them.

Model Staff Handbook (continued)

(iii) In the event of a failure to agree, the parties will consider whether conciliation or arbitration is appropriate. The Company may refer the dispute to the Advisory Conciliation and Arbitration Service, whose findings may, by mutual prior agreement, be binding on both parties.

I, *Mr. Jones* confirm that I have read and understand this Staff Handbook and accept that it forms part of my terms and conditions of employment.

....

Signed   **Dated**

APPENDIX 1

DATA PROTECTION CONSENT FORM

I hereby consent to information relating to me being processed, by the Company in order that it may properly carry out its duties, rights and obligations as my employer. I understand that such processing will principally be for personnel, administrative and payroll purposes.

I understand that information about me shall include information of a sensitive personal nature including information concerning:

[my racial or ethnic origin]

[my political opinions]

[my religious beliefs or other beliefs of a similar nature]

[my membership or non-membership of a Trade Union]

[my physical or mental health or condition]

[my sex life]

[any commission or alleged commission by me of any offence], or

[any proceedings for any offence committed or alleged to have been committed by me, the disposal of such proceedings or the sentence of any court in such proceedings].[5]

I also understand that the term 'processing' includes the obtaining, recording or holding of information or data or carrying out any operation or set of operations on the information or data, including organising, altering, retrieving, consulting, using, disclosing, combining, or destroying the information or data.

Model Staff Handbook (continued)

I confirm that I have read and understood this explanation of the processing of data relating to by the Company and that I consent to the processing of such data.

[I consent to the Company transferring the data outside of the UK for the following purposes:

[list reasons]].

.....................................Signed

....................................Dated

1 See pages 27-28 for an explanation of the rules relating to employees being laid off and guarantee payments.

Example Letter 7
Notification to employees being laid off and giving guarantee payments

Ace Fabrics Limited

16 Willow Walk, Retford, Nottingham NG6 8WS
Tel: (01777) 121211 Fax: (01777) 121233 Email: acf@uk

Dear *Miss Porter*

I refer to our meeting on *12 December 2002.*

As I explained at that meeting, we regret that because of economic pressure we have no option but to lay you off from work.

The period of lay off shall take effect from *20 December 2002* and shall continue until *20 January 2002.* You shall receive guarantee payments of £17.00 per day for the first five days of this period.[1]

I very much regret that we have been forced to take this action, but I should like to assure you that we are working hard to ensure that the period of lay off is kept to a minimum.

Yours sincerely

John Smith

John Smith
Personnel Manager

Registered Office: 16 Willow Walk, Retford, Nottingham NG6 8WS
Reg. No: England 1212298762

1 This must be no later than one month after the change to the terms of employment.

Example Letter 8
Alteration to terms of employment

Ace Fabrics Limited

16 Willow Walk, Retford, Nottingham NG6 8WS
Tel: (01777) 121211 Fax: (01777) 121233 Email: acf@uk

To: *Miss Porter*   Date: *5 February 2002*[1]
           12 Elm Drive
           Milton Keynes
           ME9 427

This letter is to let you know that the terms or conditions of your contract have been amended as set out below. If you wish to discuss any of these changes or require any further information, please let me know.

Date changes effective: *1 February 2002*

New wages/salary: *£14,000 per annum*

New hours of work: *8.30 am to 5.00 pm*

New location: *Wessex Trading Estate, High Wycombe*

Changes to duties and responsibilities: *none*

Please acknowledge receipt of this letter and your agreement to the terms set out in it by signing the attached copy of this letter and returning it to *Mr Smith*. You should retain the top copy with your contract of employment.

Signed:

....

for *Ace Fabrics Limited*

I, *Miss Porter*, acknowledge that I have received a statement of alteration to the particulars of my employment as required by the Employment Rights Act 1996 Section 1 and agree to the terms set out in that statement.

Signed: Dated:

Registered Office: 16 Willow Walk, Retford, Nottingham NG6 8WS
Reg. No: England 1212298762

Family-friendly rights

3

Chapter 3
Family-friendly rights

Employees have some important statutory rights in relation to their family responsibilities (subject to them satisfying certain qualifying conditions), which aim to strike balance between their work and home commitments. This chapter describes the various rights and is divided into sections as follows:

- Maternity rights

- Parental leave

- Time off for dependants.

Please note, however, that the law in this area regularly changes, and at the time of writing some further changes in the law are anticipated. Where possible this has been indicated in the text. In particular, measures which are due to come into force in April 2003 include:

- six months' paid and a further six months' unpaid maternity leave;

- two weeks' paid paternity leave for working fathers;

- six months' paid and a further six months' unpaid leave for adoptive parents; and

- a total increase in the rate of statutory maternity pay of £100.

MATERNITY RIGHTS

The main statutory rights that a female employee who is expecting a baby has are explained in this chapter and are as follows:

- Time off for antenatal care

- Protection from dismissal and detrimental treatment

- Suspension from work on maternity grounds

- The right to take maternity leave and return to work

- Statutory maternity pay

Time off for antenatal care

All pregnant employees are entitled to paid time off for antenatal care, irrespective of their length of service or the number of hours worked by them. This right applies only to pregnant women; husbands of pregnant women have no statutory right to attend antenatal appointments with their wives.

Except in the case of the first appointment, the employee must produce a certificate confirming her pregnancy and an appointment card or some other document showing that an appointment has been made, if requested to do so by her employer.

The actual length of absence for antenatal care must be reasonable. It may include time for travelling to and from an appointment. If an appointment lasts longer than expected, the employer should still be obliged to pay the employee for the whole of the time that was required to attend the appointment. However, employees must not abuse their right by taking more time off than is necessary.

It may be reasonable for an employer to refuse an employee time off. Such refusal is reasonable in the circumstances that the employee can arrange to have the antenatal care outside normal working hours. Therefore, part-time staff or shift workers may be able to arrange appointments outside their normal working hours. However, the timing of appointments is often outside the individual's control and, if this is so, the employee should explain this to her employer. In these circumstances, it would be unreasonable for the employer to refuse the employee time off for antenatal care during her working hours. An employer cannot require an employee who takes time off for antenatal care to make up the time later.

What care is included in the right?

Statute does not define antenatal care except that it must be on the advice of a registered medical practitioner, midwife or health visitor. As a general guideline, however, it should be assumed that standard antenatal clinic visits are covered. The number of visits required and the length of each visit depends on the medical condition of the employee concerned.

An employment tribunal has held that exercise and relaxation classes also fall within the definition of antenatal care. But such classes would have to be on the recommendation of the employee's medical advisers.

There is no right to be paid for time off for infertility treatment. However, if an individual receiving infertility treatment becomes pregnant, then she enjoys the same statutory protection as any other pregnant employee. It is likely that she would need more time off work for antenatal care and an employer would be obliged to allow her the time off as it would probably be considered reasonable.

Doctors' appointments for the purpose of ascertaining whether or not an employee is pregnant would probably be regarded as antenatal care if the employee turned out to be pregnant but, if the employee were told that she was not pregnant, she would not be covered by the statutory right.

Pay entitlement

The employee should be paid her normal hourly rate of pay by her employer during the period of time off. If the employee is paid on the basis of a fixed salary, she should be paid as usual. Where an employee is paid by the hours she works, the rate of pay is calculated by dividing the amount of one week's pay by the normal working hours in a week.

If the number of hours worked per week is irregular, they should be averaged over the previous 12 complete working weeks. If the employee has not been employed for 12 weeks, the average should be calculated on the number of normal working hours in a week which she could reasonably expect to work under her contract of employment, or from the number of hours worked by any fellow employees in comparable employment.

Some employees may have a contractual right to be paid for time off for antenatal care. There is no right to receive both the contractual pay and the statutory pay and such entitlements can be offset against each other.

Remedies

If an employee is unreasonably refused time off, she would be guilty of misconduct if she took the time off without authorisation. However, an employee may raise a complaint with an employment tribunal if:

- her employer unreasonably refuses to give her time off for antenatal care; or

- her employer fails to pay her the appropriate amount for the time taken off for the antenatal appointment.

If a complaint is upheld, the tribunal will make a declaration to that effect. Where the complaint is a refusal to allow time off, the tribunal will order that the employer pay the employee the amount of remuneration to which she would have been entitled had time off been allowed. Where the complaint is a failure to pay the whole or part of the amount due, the tribunal will order that the employer pay the amount due.

If an employer unreasonably refuses to allow an employee time off for antenatal care and she has at least one year's service, she may also claim constructive dismissal in an employment tribunal. It is automatically unfair to dismiss a woman on the ground that she took proceedings to enforce her right to time off for antenatal care or allege that such right had been infringed.

The right to time off for antenatal care should not be confused with time off for sickness during pregnancy.

Protection from dismissal and detrimental treatment

Dismissal or selection for redundancy of any woman who is pregnant, or has recently given birth, is automatically unfair regardless of her length of service or hours of work, if any of the following apply:

- The reason or principal reason for dismissal is that she is pregnant or any other reason connected with her pregnancy.

- Her maternity leave period (as defined below) is ended by her dismissal and the reason or principal reason for her dismissal is that she has given birth to a child, or any other reason connected with her having given birth to a child.

- The reason or principal reason for her dismissal, where her contract of employment was terminated at the end of her maternity leave period, is that she took, or otherwise availed herself of the benefits of maternity leave.

- The reason or principal reason for her dismissal is a requirement or recommendation to suspend her on health and safety grounds.

- The reason or principal reason for her dismissal is that she has given birth to a child, or any other reason connected with her having given birth to a child, and her contract of employment was terminated within four weeks of the end of the maternity leave period. The circumstances of termination were such that she remained incapable of work by reason of disease or other disablement and there was in force at that time, a certificate from a medical practitioner issued during the maternity leave period.

- The reason or principal reason for her dismissal is that she is redundant and her employer has not offered her suitable available alternative employment.

For further details on unfair dismissals and the remedies available for unfair dismissal see chapter 5, *Termination of employment*.

A dismissal by reason of pregnancy may also amount to direct discrimination on the grounds of sex (see chapter 4, *Discrimination*).

Employees also have the right not to be subjected to detrimental treatment on grounds of pregnancy, childbirth (where the detriment took place during ordinary or additional maternity leave period) or maternity. No qualifying service is required and employees may seek redress through an employment tribunal for infringement of this right.

An employee who is dismissed at any time during her pregnancy or maternity period is entitled to written reasons for her dismissal, regardless of length of service, without having to make a request for written reasons. An employee may raise a complaint with an employment tribunal if she is not provided with written reasons for her dismissal. If the employment tribunal finds the employer has breached this obligation unreasonably, it may make a declaration as to what it finds the employer's reasons for dismissal to have been. The employment tribunal may also award the employee a sum equivalent to two weeks' pay.

Suspension from work on maternity grounds

Under health and safety at work legislation employers have an obligation to carry out risk assessments for the safety of employees. This assessment must include any risk posed to the health and safety of a woman who is of childbearing age.

If the assessment shows that there is a risk to an employee, the employer has an obligation to take preventative or protective action. The employer may need to vary the employee's working conditions or hours of work. If this would not be reasonable or would not avoid the risk, the employee has a right to be offered any suitable alternative work which is available. If no suitable alternative work is available, the employer has a duty to suspend the employee from work for as long as necessary to avoid the risk. The employee has these rights regardless of length of service or number of hours that she works. However, to be entitled to these rights the employee must notify her employer in writing that she is pregnant, has given birth within the previous six months or is breastfeeding. Sick notes given an indication of pregnancy may amount to written notification for these purposes.

Right to suitable alternative work

Alternative work is only suitable if it is both convenient and appropriate for the employee in question and is on terms and conditions no less favourable than her normal terms and conditions.

If suitable alternative work is available but the employer fails to offer it to the employee, the employee may raise a complaint with an employment tribunal, which may award compensation.

If the employer makes an offer of suitable alternative work but the employee unreasonably refuses the offer, she loses her right to be paid remuneration for the period of suspension (as described below).

Remuneration during suspension

If an employee is suspended on maternity pay she is entitled to full pay during the period of her suspension (subject to above). In addition to the statutory right, an employee may have a *contractual* right to remuneration during maternity suspension. In these circumstances such entitlements should be offset against each other.

During the period of maternity suspension an employee retains her continuity of employment.

If an employer fails to pay an employee all or part of any money due, the employee may raise a complaint with an employment tribunal, which will award her the amount of remuneration that it finds due.

The right to take maternity leave and return to work

All employees who are expecting a baby are entitled to 18 weeks' 'ordinary maternity leave', regardless of their length of service or hours of work. Employees who are expecting a baby and have one year's continuous service with their employer by the 11th week before the expected week of childbirth are entitled to 'additional maternity leave' of up to 29 weeks, beginning with the week the child is born. Employees who have taken ordinary maternity leave or additional maternity leave normally have the right to return to the same job.

These rights to ordinary maternity leave and additional maternity leave apply where a woman gives birth to a living child or has a still birth after 24 weeks of pregnancy.

Ordinary Maternity Leave

(i) **Duration**

Maternity leave may not commence before the start of the 11th week before the beginning of the week in which the baby is due. Subject to this, maternity leave begins on the date the employee tells her employer she intends her leave to start. However, maternity leave can begin earlier than the date the employee chooses if she is absent from work for a reason which is wholly or partly because of her pregnancy. The Department of Social Security publishes a free leaflet *Pregnancy related illnesses*, NI200, which sets out the illnesses which are recognised as being connected to pregnancy. In these circumstances, her maternity leave shall begin on the first day of her absence, provided that date is after the beginning of the sixth week before the start of the week the baby is due.

In most circumstances maternity leave ends 18 weeks after it begins. However, women are prohibited from working within two weeks of childbirth. If a child is born later than expected and the two weeks following childbirth do not fall within the 18-week maternity leave period, then the period may be extended by up to two weeks. It is a criminal offence for an employer to fail to comply with this prohibition.

(ii) **Notification**

Currently an employee is only entitled to maternity leave if she gives the required notice verbally or in writing of:

- the fact that she is pregnant;

- the expected week her baby is due (or the date of the birth in the unlikely event that it has already occurred); and

- the date she wishes her leave to begin.

Notification must be given at least 21 days before the maternity leave period commences or, if that is not possible, as soon as is reasonably practicable thereafter. In addition to compulsory notification and if the employer so requests, the employee must produce a certificate from a registered medical practitioner or midwife stating the expected week the baby is due.

If the maternity leave period has started before the notified leave date, either due to pregnancy-related absence or the employee giving birth, the employee must notify her employer as soon as she can that she is absent for whatever reason. If the employer requests, this notification must be in writing.

(iii) **Rights during maternity leave**

During maternity leave an employee is entitled to all the benefits that she would have received had she not been on maternity leave, except remuneration. This means that the contract of employment continues and the period on maternity leave counts towards her continuity of employment.

(iv) **Contractual rights**

It is not uncommon for an employee's employment contract to grant more favourable maternity provisions than the statutory rights.

Additional Maternity Leave

(i) **Duration**

Ordinary and additional maternity leave together may last up to 40 weeks (11 weeks before the expected week of childbirth and 29 weeks after the actual week of birth).

(ii) **Notification**

No notice needs to be given by the employee of her intentions to take additional maternity leave. It is presumed she will take it unless she notifies otherwise.

(iii) **Rights during additional maternity leave**

The contract of employment continues during the additional maternity leave period but the only terms and conditions that need apply will be the employers obligations of trust and confidence and the employees obligations of good faith and any terms and conditions relating to notice of termination of the employee contract by the employer or the employee, compensation in the event of redundancy, disciplinary or grievance procedures, disclosure of confidential information, the acceptance by the employee of gifts or other benefits or her participation in any other business.

Right to return to work

(i) **Ordinary maternity leave**

An employee returning after 18 weeks' ordinary maternity leave normally has the right to return to the same job that she left. If she wants to return to work before the end of her 18-week leave she must give her employer at least 21 days' notice of the date she intends to return to work.

(ii) **Additional maternity leave**

An employee returning after additional maternity leave has the right to return to work of the same nature, capacity and location, at the rate of pay which she would have received had she not been absent at all, and on terms and conditions which are no less favourable than those which would have applied had she not been absent from work after the end of her additional maternity leave.

There are circumstances when the employer may offer suitable and appropriate alternative work if it is not reasonably practicable to allow the employee to return to work.

Where the employee has not been in touch to notify the date of the birth, the employer may write no earlier than 21 days before the end of the ordinary maternity leave seeking confirmation of the date of birth and her intention to return. The employee must respond within 21 days of receiving the request. Where the employee fails to respond, she does not lose her right to return to work but the employer can take appropriate disciplinary action.

If the employer refuses to allow a woman to return from maternity leave she will be entitled to claim unfair dismissal. Case law would suggest a claim of sex discrimination may also be successful in these circumstances.

Employees who have taken ordinary maternity leave or additional maternity leave are increasingly likely to ask to return on a part-time basis, or even to switch to working from home. For both types of leave the entitlement is actually to return to the job she left, i.e. a full-time one. However, the employer must consider such requests carefully. If a part-time job or homeworking is not a viable option, a full explanation must be given showing grounds on which refusal can be justified. An unjustifiable refusal to offer part-time work or homeworking can result in a successful claim of indirect sex discrimination, on the basis that the requirement to work full-time is one that fewer women than men can comply with because of family responsibilities.

Employees are entitled not to be subjected to any detriment by any act or omission of their employer due to the fact they are pregnant, have given birth to a child, have been suspended from work on maternity grounds, took or availed herself of the benefits of ordinary or additional maternity leave.

There is no right for the employee to postpone the return to work after additional maternity leave if she is unfit to return to work. If the employee is sick, the normal company rules on sick leave will apply.

Statutory maternity pay

Statutory maternity pay (SMP) is a payment that employers are required to make to eligible employees, even if the employee does not intend to return to work after the child is born.

Eligibility

An employee only qualifies for SMP if:

- she has stopped work wholly or partly because of pregnancy or childbirth; and

- she has 6 months' continuous employment with the same employer by the start of the 14th week before the expected week of childbirth; and

- her normal weekly earnings in the eight weeks before the start of the 14th week before the expected week of childbirth were above the lower earnings limit for the payment of National Insurance contributions, currently £75 (if the employee's normal weekly earnings are below the lower earnings limit, she can apply for maternity allowance from the DSS on Form SMP1); and

- she has reached the start of the 11th week before the expected week of childbirth (or if before, she has given birth).

Entitlement

The employee is entitled to SMP for 18 weeks (known as the 'maternity pay period') as follows:

- for the first six weeks, 90% of her normal weekly earnings over a reference period of eight weeks immediately before the 14th week before the expected week of childbirth;

- for the rest of the maternity pay period, a flat rate of £75 per week.

SMP is subject to income tax, National Insurance contributions and any other regular deductions and should be paid by the same method and at the same time as the employee would normally be paid. If there is no normal agreement as to which day wages are paid on, payment should be made on the last day of the calendar month.

Employers also need to ensure SMP is calculated, or adjusted, to take account of any salary increase received between the start of the reference period and the end of the period when the employee is in receipt of the higher rate of SMP.

The employee may also have a contractual right to maternity pay which the employer may set off against SMP.

How to make a claim for SMP

To make a claim, the employee simply gives her employer 21 days' notification that she will be absent because of her pregnancy or as much notice as is practicable. The employer may request this notice be in writing and then is obliged to complete various forms. The Government-run Employer's Helpline can provide further details on 0845 714 3143.

If the employee gives birth before the date notified or before the 14th week before the expected week of childbirth, she must give notice stating that her absence is due to the birth, within 21 days of the birth, or as soon as is reasonably practicable thereafter. In this notice she must specify the date of the birth of her child and the date her absence began. The employer may request this notice in writing.

The employee is not required to give notice if she leaves the job for a reason wholly unconnected with her pregnancy after the beginning of the 15th week before the expected week of childbirth. She must, however, give her employer notice of the date on which she actually went into labour if this fell before the 11th week before the expected week of childbirth.

The employee must also provide her employer with a maternity certificate completed by a doctor or registered midwife as evidence of her pregnancy and expected week of childbirth.

Remedies for non-payment of SMP

If the employer fails to pay SMP or the employee disputes the amount paid, the employee has the right to require from her employer a written statement of what SMP it considers to be due and reasons why.

If nothing is resolved, the matter may be referred to an adjudication officer. An appeal from the adjudication officer's decision may be made to the Social Security Appeals Tribunal and a further appeal lies on a point of law only to the Social Security Commissioners.

Reclaiming SMP

The employer may reclaim at least 92 per cent of the gross amount of SMP it has paid by deducting it from the total (i.e. both primary and secondary) Class 1 national insurance contributions due to be paid for all employees in that tax month.

Small employers whose annual gross national insurance bill does not exceed £20,000 are entitled to recover 100 per cent of SMP paid, plus additional compensation of 4.5 per cent of total SMP paid.

1 Not to be sent before
21 days before the end of
the ordinary maternity leave
(see page 83).

Example Letter 9
Requesting confirmation of return to work after maternity absence[1]

Ace Fabrics Limited

16 Willow Walk, Retford, Nottingham NG6 8WS
Tel: (01777) 121211 Fax: (01777) 121233 Email: acf@uk

Dear *Jenny*,

I should like to express my congratulations to you on the birth of your baby.

I expect that you have now had time to consider your position. Therefore, I would like to know if you are still intending to return to work on or before *10 October 2002*.

Please respond within 21 days of receipt of this letter. If you do not respond within this time, you will not lose your right to return to work, but the Company may take appropriate disciplinary action.

I look forward to hearing from you shortly, but if you have any queries please do not hesitate to contact me.

Yours sincerely

John Smith

John Smith
Personnel Manager

Registered Office: 16 Willow Walk, Retford, Nottingham NG6 8WS
Tel: (01777) 121211 Fax: (01777) 121233
Reg. No: England 1212298762

PARENTAL LEAVE

Employees have a right to take 13 weeks unpaid leave for the purposes of caring for a child subject to satisfying certain qualified conditions.

What is parental leave?

Parental leave may be taken not just in connection with caring for a child's health. For example, it can be used for the purposes of settling the child into a playgroup, taking a child on holiday or simply staying at home with the child.

Qualifying conditions

A person qualifies for the right to parental leave if they are an employee with at least one year's continuous service and have or expect to have responsibility for a child. A person has responsibility for a child in the following circumstances:

- they are the natural mother or father who were married at the time of birth;

- they are the natural mother where the parents are not married at time of birth;

- they are the natural father where the parents were not married at the time of birth if the father acquires parental responsibility by court order or agreement with the mother;

- they are a legal guardian;

- they are an adoptive parent.

The relevant child must have been under 5 on 15 December 1999 or if the child is an adopted child, the child must have been adopted after 15 December 1994.

It is a fundamental principal that the right to parental leave is an individual one and will be non-transferable. This means that both parents will be able to take up to 13 weeks leave if they are both working, but they will not be able to add their leave entitlement so that one employee can take more than 13 weeks and the other less.

This is clearly designed to encourage fathers to take parental leave. If a man does not use his leave, it will simply go to waste.

When can parental leave be taken?

Parental leave may be taken before the child's 5th birthday or where they have been adopted for a period of five years or up to the age of 18, whichever is the sooner. An exception to this is where the employer has postponed parental leave in such circumstances it would be possible to have the postponed leave taken after the 5th birthday or anniversary of adoption cut-off point. Also where a child is entitled to a disability living allowance, parental leave may be taken at any time up until the child's 18th birthday. Parental leave may not be taken in periods of less than a week and any fraction of a week will be treated as a whole week. The exception to this is in cases where the child is entitled to a disability living allowance.

Rights during parental leave

The employment relationship continues during the leave period although leave may be unpaid. The employment relationship continues in exactly the same way as in the case of a person taking maternity leave, namely, the employee is entitled to the benefit of his or her employer's implied obligation to her of trust and confidence and is also bound by his or her implied obligation of good faith and any express obligation prohibiting disclosure of confidential information or the employee's participation in any competing business.

Right to return to work

Employees taking parental leave for a period of more than 4 weeks or immediately after additional maternity leave have the right to return to his or her old job at the end of the leave period. Alternatively if it is not reasonably practicable for him or her to return to his or her old job, he or she has the right to return to another job which is both suitable for the individual and appropriate to do in the circumstances. The terms and conditions on which the individual may return to work after parental leave are as follows:

- on terms and conditions as to remuneration no less favourable than those which would have been applicable to him or her had they not been absent from work;

- with seniority, pension rights and similar rights as they would have been if the period prior to his or her parental leave period were continuous with his or her employment following his or her return to work; and

- otherwise on terms and conditions no less favourable than those which have been applicable to him or her or he or she not been absent from work during the period or parental leave.

Parental leave schemes

The Government has indicated that it would like employers to agree its own parental leave schemes which suits the needs of its business and employees. However, in order to implement a legally enforceable parental scheme it is necessary for this to be entered into by way of a collective agreement or a work force agreement. A collective agreement is one which is reached between the union and an employer as a result of collective bargaining. A workforce agreement is, in effect, a sort of collective agreement which does not involve a union as such. It is an agreement between an employer and his workers which satisfies certain conditions. It has to be in writing and cannot have effect for more than five years. It has to apply to all members of the workforce or all members of the workforce who belong to a particular group. It has to be signed either by representatives of the workforce or group or, where there are 20 or fewer employees, by appropriate representatives or the majority of the employees. This is a fairly complex procedure and it is therefore recommended that if the employer wishes to implement its own parental leave scheme by means of a workforce agreement, further advice should be sought.

If the employer does not implement its own parental leave scheme, the legislation provides that default provisions automatically come into play. These provide that an employee can only exercise his or her entitlement to parental leave if:
- he or she has complied with a reasonable request made the employer to produce evidence of entitlement to take parental leave and the child's date of birth or the date on which a placement began for an adopted child;
- he has given his or her employer proper notice; and

- the employer does not postpone the leave period.

The amount of notice which the employee must give the employer before taking parental leave is 21 days. When leave is to begin either on the birth of a child or the placement of a child for adoption the notice must be given at least 21 days before the beginning of the expected week of childbirth or week of placement. The default provisions also provide that an employee may not take more than 4 weeks' leave in respect of any individual child during a 12 month period.

Postponement of parental leave

The employer can postpone when a period of parental leave may be taken except where this is to be taken on the birth or placement of a child. In every other circumstance the employer can postpone parental leave if the employer considers that the operation of the business would be unduly disrupted. The employer must agree to allow the employee to take the same period of leave within at least six months. To postpone, the employer must give notice within 7 days after the employee's notice requesting leave was given to the employer.

Enforcement

An employee has a right to make a claim in the employment tribunal if his employer unreasonably postpones or refuses to attempts to prevent the grant of parental leave. Compensation is such as the tribunal considers just and equitable taking into account the employers behaviour and the loss sustained by the employee as a result of the matter complained of.

Employees also have protection from being subjected to any detriment by any act or omission by the employer because they took or sought to take parental leave. The employee also has protection of automatic unfair dismissal if they are dismissed for a reason relating to the fact that they took parental leave.

There is no statutory requirement for an employer to keep records of when parental leave has been taken. In practice, it is highly likely that organisations will need to keep some sort of record. When an employee changes employers he or she will need to requalify and has no right to take more than 13 weeks for each child in total, including any leave that may have been taken with the previous employer.

Therefore it will be sensible when requesting a reference from a previous employer to ask them to provide details of whether parental leave has been taken by the individual, and if so how much.

TIME OFF FOR DEPENDANTS

All employees (regardless of service) are entitled to take a reasonable amount of unpaid leave to deal with incidents involving a dependant.

Dependants are defined as the employee's parent, wife, husband or partner, child or someone who lives as part of the family. The employee has the right to time off:

- to help when a dependant is ill or injured;
- to cope when the arrangements for caring for a dependant unexpectedly break down;
- when a dependant gives birth;
- when a dependant dies; or
- to deal with unexpected incident involving a dependent child during school hours, or on a school trip.

In the first two cases, the dependant could also be someone who relies on the employee in the particular emergency.

No predetermined maximum is set on the amount of time off which can be taken. However, it is envisaged by the Government that one or two days will usually be the most that are needed to deal with the immediate issues and sort out longer term arrangements if necessary.

An employee may complain to an employment tribunal if his or her employer unreasonably refuses to permit him or her to take time off for dependants. If the tribunal find the complaint well founded, compensation may be awarded such as the tribunal considers just and equitable in all these circumstances having regard to the employers default and any loss sustained by the employee which is attributable to the matters complained of.

Employees also have protection from detriment by any act or omission by the employer because they took or sought to take time off for dependants.

Discrimination

Chapter 4
Discrimination

What you'll find in this chapter:

⟱ Sex discrimination and discrimination on the grounds of marriage

⟱ Race discrimination

⟱ Equal pay

⟱ Disability discrimination

⟱ Harassment

The law on discrimination has an enormous effect in employment. The UK's membership in the European Union (EU) means that a high level of protection from discrimination exists for employees. An employee who complains of discrimination in whatever way can pursue legal action in an employment tribunal and no qualifying period is necessary in order to bring such a claim. Discrimination claims are not subject to any maximum award and are therefore increasing in number and value.

UK legislation that governs discrimination complies with the EU law, when new EU laws are introduced UK laws must be amended accordingly.

There is currently protection from discrimination in relation to sex, marital status, gender re-assignment, race, trade union membership and disability.

There is currently no law against treating employees or prospective employees less favourably because of their age, although a voluntary Code of Practice has recently been issued to tackle the problem of age discrimination. In addition, restrictions on age can in some circumstances amount to indirect sex discrimination (see below).

Although there has been much pressure in the UK for a law to protect homosexuals being discriminated against on the grounds of their sexual preference, nothing as yet has been enacted. EU law as it currently stands, offers no protection and no remedy. However, it is worth noting that the new human rights legislation has been used in this area to attempt to interpret the word 'sex' in the Sex Discrimination Act to include 'sexual orientation'. Although the tribunal in Scotland accepted this and found that an employee dismissed because he was homosexual had been discriminated against, this case has now been overturned.

Sex discrimination and discrimination on the grounds of marriage

Discrimination on the grounds of sex or marriage is made unlawful by the Sex Discrimination Act 1975 (SDA) which forbids it at every stage of employment (i.e. advertising vacancies, engagement of employees, promotion, training and other opportunities, and dismissal). Employment has a wider definition in the SDA than other employment protection legislation, protecting not only individuals who are employees but also individuals working under a contract for services and partners in a partnership. In addition, other organisations, including trade unions, trade or professional associations and employment agencies must also observe the provisions of the SDA.

Individuals who are not protected by the SDA in their employment are:

- persons who work wholly or mainly outside Great Britain;

- police officers in relation to height requirements and uniform or uniform allowances;

- prison officers in relation to height requirements;

- ministers of religion if employment is limited to one sex in order to comply with the doctrines of the religion or to avoid offending the religious sensibilities of a significant number of its followers.

Definition of discrimination

DEFINITION

There are three recognised forms of discrimination:

(a)   direct discrimination

(b)   indirect discrimination

(c)   victimisation

In deciding whether discrimination has occurred, the position of the person allegedly discriminated against is compared to that of a person of similar skill and qualification. The intention or motive of the alleged discriminator is irrelevant. The SDA protects males as well as females.

(a)   Direct discrimination

DEFINITION

Direct discrimination is easy to recognise: it occurs where an employee has received less favourable treatment and would not have but for his or her sex or marital status. For there to be direct discrimination, the person's sex or marital status is the basis of the particular decision which results in the individual being deprived in some way and which gives rise to less favourable treatment. It is the treatment itself rather than its consequences which must be different and less favourable.

An individual may exercise unconscious prejudices, because of his or her upbringing and perceptions, without being aware of the fact and this can amount to direct discrimination. It is important that employers give training in order to avoid such prejudices.

The burden of proof for direct discrimination involves the individual complaining of discrimination having to bring evidence that would lead the tribunal to presume or infer there has been discrimination. It will then be up to the employer to disprove this inference or presumption.

Dress requirements. The test of whether or not the individual would have received the same treatment, but for his or her sex, has proved problematic where the treatment complained of is the imposition of dress requirement. Therefore, there is no discrimination where male and female employees are subject to different but comparable dress requirements.

Maternity cases. Unfavourable treatment on the grounds of an employee's pregnancy or for other maternity-related reasons is direct discrimination contrary to the SDA. There is no need for a comparison with a male employee: once a female employee has established that her treatment amounted to direct discrimination, no question of justification for this treatment can arise.

This occurs when a woman is engaged by the employer for an indefinite period. However, if a woman is employed for a single fixed-term period or to fulfil a particular task, it is uncertain whether the employer would be guilty of discrimination if the woman was denied employment during which time she would be unavailable for work because of her pregnancy or, if after engaging the woman for such a period, the employer discovered that she was pregnant and subsequently cancelled the agreement.

(b) **Indirect discrimination**

DEFINITION

Indirect discrimination covers other forms of less obvious discriminatory treatment. Indirect discrimination takes place where:

- an employer imposes a condition or requirement with which the individual cannot comply and which is to his or her detriment;

- the condition or requirement can be shown to have a disproportionate impact in excluding others of the individual's sex or marital status; and

- the condition cannot be justified, irrespective of the individual's sex or marital status.

Please note that there is no requirement for the individual to show that they cannot comply with the condition, requirement, provision, criterion or practice, they just need to show it is to their detriment.

For example, indirect sex discrimination would take place where an employer imposed a requirement for all employees to be subject to a five foot maximum height requirement. A much larger proportion of women than men would be able to meet this requirement and the employer would have to justify the reason for imposing such a condition. If the reason was because the job was to crew a boat with very low ceilings such a requirement would probably be justified. But, if the reason was because the employer only wished to provide one size of uniform, the employer would be indirectly discriminating against men.

Justification requires an objective balance between the discriminatory effect of the condition or requirement and the reasonable needs of the employer who is applying it. Justification is a 'matter of fact' for the employment tribunal, which means that one tribunal might reach one conclusion and another might reach a different conclusion.

Age. Although there is no law against age discrimination, placing restrictions on age can, in some circumstances, amount to indirect sex discrimination. This has been the case where an employer required a maximum age limit of 28 for a job. An employment appeal tribunal held this was indirectly discriminatory because in practice it was harder for women to comply with it than men, since women in their 20s are commonly fully occupied with child-bearing.

(c)   **Victimisation**

An employer would be guilty of sex discrimination by victimisation if it treated any employee less favourably than others because that employee had brought, or threatened to bring proceedings, give evidence or information, or take any action or make any allegation concerning the employer, with reference to the SDA or the Equal Pay Act 1970 (EPA).

Exceptions to sex discrimination protection

The law recognises that there are some circumstances where there may be a good reason to give favourable treatment to a particular sex. In particular, there are two areas:

- **Positive discrimination**. If an employer identifies that one sex is not properly represented within certain work areas, it may try to encourage individuals of that particular sex to apply, by providing training or through an advertising campaign. Before doing this, the employer must be able to show that in the previous 12 months there have been either no individuals of that particular sex, or only a small proportion of them, carrying out the work in question. If not, the positive action will be discriminatory.

- **Genuine occupational qualifications**. For some jobs being of a certain sex is a requirement, as set out in chapter 1. But attitudes and cultures are changing and an exception which was once acceptable may no longer be so. The applicability of the genuine occupational qualification exception should be considered every time a vacancy is advertised.

Employer responsibility for discrimination

Under the SDA an employer is liable for anything done by his employees in the course of their employment, whether or not it was done with the employer's knowledge or approval. This ensures that the employer takes responsibility for preventing discrimination at work (in the SDA 'employment' has a wide definition and includes any contract personally to execute work and is not confined to a contract of service). However, it is a defence if the employer can prove that he took such steps as were practicable to prevent an employee from doing a certain act.

If the employer wishes to rely on this defence, it must be shown that positive steps have been taken to address the possibility of discrimination occurring in the work place. For example, the employer should introduce and adhere to an equal opportunities policy which incorporates a sexual and racial harassment policy (see the model equal opportunities clause included in the Staff Handbook on page 59). All employees should be aware of such policies and be given training in their obligations not to discriminate. Disciplinary action should be taken against those who do discriminate.

The individual discriminator still risks that action will be taken against him or her whether or not the employer is found responsible. An individual who wishes to pursue an action for discrimination may issue proceedings in an employment tribunal against his or her employer and against the individual discriminator. However, if the individual discriminator can prove that the action taken was based on an assurance from the employer that it was not discriminatory, he or she will not be held liable for discrimination.

Other unlawful acts under the SDA

It is unlawful to do any of the following:

- to knowingly aid and abet someone in unlawful discrimination; the person who committed the discriminatory act has the defence that he or she acted reasonably, relying on a statement by the other that the act would not be unlawful;

- to instruct someone to discriminate over whom one has authority or to someone who normally acts in accordance with one's wishes;

- to induce or attempt to induce someone to discriminate; such inducements may include offering either benefits or detriments.

No contracting-out

Employers are not allowed to exclude or limit any provision of the SDA in a contract of employment. If they do it would have no effect, leaving the employee at liberty to bring a complaint under the SDA against the employer in an employment tribunal.

The Equal Opportunities Commission (EOC)

The SDA establishes the EOC, which has the following duties:

- to work towards the elimination of discrimination;

- to promote equality of opportunity between men and women generally; and

- to keep under review the work of the SDA and the EPA (for more details on the EPA see page 109).

Codes of Practice. The EOC has issued a code of practice and guidance notes for the elimination of sex and marriage discrimination and the promotion of equality of opportunity in employment. Employers are advised to review the code and guidance notes and to put into place its recommendations. A breach of the recommendations does not of itself render a person liable to proceedings, but it may be taken into account by an employment tribunal when determining whether or not discrimination has occurred.

Investigations. As part of its general duties, the EOC may if it thinks fit, and if required by the Secretary of State for Education and Employment, conduct a formal investigation, (which may be in relation to a particular organisation), where it considers there has been a breach of the provisions of the SDA or the EPA.

Non-discrimination notice. The EOC can issue a non-discrimination notice if it finds that a person has committed or is committing an unlawful discriminatory act or practice, a breach of the provisions relating to advertising, or of a term modified (or included) by virtue of an equality clause or has given instructions to discriminate or pressure to discriminate. This notice may require a person to stop committing any such acts, or to change any of his or her practices or arrangements, to inform the EOC that he or she has effected those changes and what they are, and to take such steps to inform people affected by those practices or arrangements. The EOC cannot issue a non-discrimination notice without (i) informing the relevant person of its intention and the grounds of the notice, (ii) allowing the relevant person at least 28 days in which to make representations and (iii) taking into account all the representations made by him.

Employers are advised to ensure that they do not breach any of the provisions of the SDA or the EPA. If they do, and are informed of a proposal to issue a notice, they must take action to prevent the discrimination. If a notice has been issued and the employers do not wish to challenge it, they should comply with it as soon as possible. An employer has a right of appeal against any requirement of a non-discrimination notice.

A register of non-discrimination notices which have been issued is available for inspection and for copying from the Equal Opportunities Commission, listed in the Appendix.

Gender re-assignment

The SDA also prohibits direct discrimination on the ground that a person intends to undergo, is undergoing or has undergone a sex change. There is no protection against indirect discrimination.

As with claims of sex discrimination, an allegation of gender re-assignment discrimination will not succeed if the defendant can show that a genuine occupational qualification applies, so as to justify the discrimination. The genuine occupational qualifications are those set out in chapter 1, with some further supplementary genuine occupational qualifications created specifically to cover gender re-assignment discrimination.

Race discrimination

Discrimination on racial grounds is made unlawful by the Race Relations Act 1976 (RRA) which reflects many of the principles and rules contained in the SDA examined in the first section of this chapter. The RRA forbids less favourable treatment of individuals on racial grounds at every stage of employment. Like the SDA, the RRA protects not only individual employees but also individuals working under a contract for services and partners in a partnership (where the partnership consists of six or more partners). In addition, trade unions, trade or professional associations, employment agencies and other organisations must also observe the provisions of the RRA.

Individuals not protected by the RRA are:

- those who work wholly or mainly outside Great Britain;

- individuals employed by a private household (with the exception of discrimination by victimisation, see page 107).

Definition of race discrimination

DEFINITION

The three forms of discrimination in relation to sex and on the grounds of marriage apply equally to race. Whereas the definitions of sex and marriage are straightforward, what is meant by racial grounds requires further explanation. If a decision is based on an individual's colour, race, nationality or national origins, or ethnic origins it is a decision based on racial grounds and could be discriminatory.

The meaning of 'ethnic origins' needs clarifying. It has been held that a group has an ethnic origin if it has certain characteristics:

- a long shared history; and

- a cultural tradition.

Additional relevant characteristics are:

- a common geographical origin or descent from a small number of common ancestors;

- a common language not necessarily peculiar to the group;

- a common literature peculiar to the group;

- a common religion different from that of the neighbouring or surrounding community;

- being a minority or being in an oppressed or dominant group in a large community.

It has been held in the courts that Sikhs are an ethnic group, as are Jews and Gypsies, but at present Rastafarians have been held not to fall within what can be considered an ethnic group.

In a sex discrimination claim a comparison is made between a female employee and a male employee in equivalent circumstances to decide whether the treatment of one is less favourable. In a race discrimination claim, the comparison must be between the person of the racial or ethnic group and a job applicant or employee who is not of that ethnic or racial group, but whose circumstances are the same, similar or not materially different.

The burden of proof in race discrimination claims differs slightly to the burden of proof in sex discrimination claims. The individual complaining of race discrimination must establish the case and then the employer has to justify the alleged discriminatory act. If no explanation is forthcoming or an unsatisfactory explanation is provided, then the employment tribunal is entitled to infer that discrimination did in fact take place.

(a) **Direct discrimination**

The principle of direct discrimination as already examined in relation to sex and marriage discrimination, applies here: in a race discrimination claim the less favourable treatment is obviously on racial grounds and the test is whether, but for the individual's racial origin, ethnic origin, nationality, national origin or colour, he or she would not have been subject to that treatment.

(b) **Indirect discrimination**

Broadly, the principle of indirect discrimination as examined in relation to sex and marriage discrimination applies to race discrimination. However, there are some differences. Indirect discrimination will occur if a condition or requirement is imposed which has a disproportionate impact on a particular racial group so that a considerably smaller proportion of members of that group can comply than those outside it, and it cannot be objectively justified on some basis other than colour, race, nationality or ethnic or national origins.

Whether someone can comply with a condition or requirement is decided by what he or she can do in practice rather than in theory.

The question of whether indirect discrimination is objectively justifiable is (as with sex and marriage discrimination) one of fact for an employment tribunal. The employment tribunal must strike a balance between the discriminatory effect of the condition or requirement being imposed and the reasonable needs of the employer applying it.

(c) **Victimisation**

An employer would be guilty of race discrimination by victimisation if he or she treated any employee less favourably than others because that employee has already or threatens to bring proceedings, give evidence or information, take any action or make any allegation concerning the employer with reference to the RRA.

Exceptions to race discrimination protection

As with sex discrimination, the law recognises that in some circumstances there may be a good reason to give favourable treatment to a particular race. There are two areas where exceptions to the law against race discrimination exist:

- **Positive discrimination**. If an employer identifies a particular racial group as not being properly represented within certain work areas, he may try to encourage individuals of that group to apply by providing training or through an advertising campaign. The employer must be able to show that in the previous 12 months there have been either no individuals of the racial group or only a small proportion of them carrying out the particular work in question. If this exception does not apply then the positive action will be discriminatory. A booklet entitled *What is Positive Action?* published by the Race Relations Employment Advisory Service provides further explanation of positive race discrimination.

- **Genuine occupational qualifications**. For some jobs belonging to a certain racial group is a requirement, as set out in chapter 1. The number of jobs where a person's race is a genuine occupational qualification is not as high as that concerning a person's sex. The warning that attitudes and cultures are changing should also be remembered in relation to race. The applicability of the genuine occupational qualification exception should be considered every time a vacancy is advertised.

Employer responsibility for race discrimination

The same principle applies under the RRA as previously described in relation to the SDA in the first section of this chapter. For an employer relying on this defence, regard will be given to whether a written policy on race discrimination has been issued to employees, whether training has been given and whether disciplinary action has been taken against those guilty of race discrimination.

Other unlawful acts under the RRA

The unlawful acts listed on pages 102-103 in relation to the SDA equally apply to the RRA.

No contracting-out

The ban on contractual clauses excluding or limiting provisions of the SDA equally applies to excluding or limiting those of the RRA.

The Commission for Racial Equality (CRE)

The RRA establishes the CRE, which has the following duties:

- to work towards the elimination of discrimination;

- to promote equality of opportunity between persons of different racial groups;

- to keep under review the working of the RRA.

These duties are the same as the duties of the EOC in relation to sex discrimination and the points previously made about codes of practice, investigations and non-discrimination notices apply equally to the CRE. The address of the CRE is listed in the Appendix.

Equal pay

The Equal Pay Act 1970 (EPA) provides that discrimination between the sexes in the terms of their contracts of employment is unlawful. This typically occurs in matters such as salary, bonus payments and benefits.

The EPA has been criticised because its provisions are too complex and it takes many years for claims under the Act to reach a conclusion.

The EPA protects males as well as females and it benefits employees under a contract of employment as well as self-employed people under a contract for services. It does not apply to individuals who work wholly or mainly outside Great Britain nor does it apply to members of the armed forces.

The EOC has recently published a Code of Practice on Pay which aims to provide practical guidance on good practice in relation to equal pay, which includes a suggested equal pay policy.

DEFINITION

Meaning of equality

An individual can claim equality if he or she can establish one of the following:

- that he or she is carrying out work which is the same or broadly similar to work being carried out by someone of the opposite sex in the same employment; or

- that he or she is carrying out work which has been rated as equal, through a job evaluation study, to work being carried out by someone of the opposite sex in the same employment; or

- that he or she is carrying out work which is of equal value to the work of someone of the opposite sex in the same employment.

Comparison. The comparison must be with a person of the opposite sex who exists (or has existed) who is doing like work, work graded as equal or work of equal value and who is employed by the same employer (or an associated employer) either at the same establishment or at an establishment within Great Britain where, in general, common terms and conditions are observed.

Defence. An employer can successfully defend a claim under the EPA if it can:

- prove that the work is not like or similar, not rated as equal or not of equal value; or

- prove that the difference between the complainant's contract and the comparison contract is genuinely due to a material factor which is not the difference in sex; this requires that the employer show the reason for the factor and that the factor identified objectively justifies the difference in the contracts.

Equality clause. If an individual can establish that one of the above three justifications for equality applies and his or her contract contains terms less beneficial than those enjoyed by the comparator of the opposite sex, or which omits a beneficial term enjoyed by the comparator, he or she can apply to an employment tribunal to have an equality clause implied into his or her contract. Such a clause modifies the individual's contract so that it is equivalent to the comparator's contract.

Other remedies. In addition to an equality clause in the contract, a person successful in a complaint under the EPA may be awarded compensation for loss suffered in the past as a result of lack of equality.

Disability discrimination

Discrimination on the grounds of disability is made unlawful by the Disability Discrimination Act 1996 (DDA). Breach of the DDA can result in a complaint to an employment tribunal with no limit to the amount of compensation. The Government has produced information booklets on different sections of the DDA; these and the Code of Practice are available by calling 0845 762 2633.

The main consequence of the DDA is that it is now unlawful for an employer of 15 or more employees to discriminate against a disabled person – or someone who has been disabled in the past – in recruitment, terms and conditions of employment, promotion, training (or other benefits), dismissal or by subjecting him or her to any disadvantage. It is important that the term 'employees' be widely interpreted to included the self-employed and those engaged under a contract of service or apprenticeship (as it is with other discrimination legislation). The provisions of the DDA do not currently apply to employers of fewer than 15 people, although this exemption is due to be abolished in 2004, and there are some categories of employees to whom they do not apply.

Code of Practice

This gives practical guidance to employers on fulfilling their new obligations and avoiding possible claims of discrimination. Breaches of the Code are admissible as evidence in employment tribunal hearings.

What kind of discrimination is covered by the DDA?

A disability is defined in this context as a physical or mental impairment which has a substantial and long-term adverse effect on a person's ability to carry out normal day-to-day activities. Such a broad definition includes learning disabilities, mental illnesses (if recognised by a respected body of medical opinion), impairments which come and go if the actual effect is likely to recur (e.g. rheumatoid arthritis) and severe disfigurements. People with progressive conditions are covered from the moment the condition leads to impairment of their ability to carry out day-to-day activities. The definition specifically excludes some impairments, such as alcohol or drug addiction, hayfever and self-disfigurement (i.e. tattoos).

What is discrimination in this context?

DEFINITION

An employer discriminates against a disabled person if:

- it treats him or her less favourably, for a reason related to the person's present or past disability, than it treats or would treat a person to whom that reason does not apply and the employer cannot show that this treatment is justified;

- it fails to comply with a new duty of making reasonable adjustments in relation to disabled persons, and the employer cannot show that this failure is justified.

Justification

Less favourable treatment of a disabled person is justified if the reason for it is both 'material' to the circumstances of the case and 'substantial'. According to the code this means that the reason has to relate to the individual circumstances in question and must not be trivial or minor. The code gives some examples, including these:

1. Someone who is blind is not shortlisted for a job involving computers because the employer thinks blind people cannot use them. The employer makes no effort to consider the individual circumstances. This general assumption that blind people cannot use computers would not in itself be a material (i.e. justified) reason because it is not related to the particular circumstances of the applicant.

2. Someone who has psoriasis (a skin condition) is rejected for a job involving modelling cosmetics on a part of the body which, in his case, is severely disfigured by the condition. This would be justified if his appearance were incompatible with the purpose of the work. The reason is material to the individual circumstances of the case and it is substantial.

Employers may offer a disabled person less favourable terms of employment if there is a material and substantial reason for doing so and no reasonable adjustments can be made to remove that reason. For example, if, despite any reasonable adjustments, a disabled employee has a significantly lower output than other employees the employer can pay that employee less than the others.

Reasonable adjustments

If any physical feature of the employer's premises or other arrangements causes a substantial disadvantage to a disabled person, the employer must make reasonable adjustments to prevent it. 'Arrangements' includes all that an employer arranges in recruiting employees and in the workplace, for example selection and interview procedures and working conditions.

Appropriate adjustments might include altering premises, re-allocating duties, transferring staff to fill an existing vacancy, altering working hours, assigning someone to a different place of work, allowing absences from office training, acquiring or modifying equipment, modifying instructions or manuals, modifying procedures for testing or assessment and providing a reader or supervision. Whether it is reasonable for an employer to have to make a particular adjustment will depend upon a number of factors:

- how effective it would be in preventing the disadvantage

- how practical it is

- the financial and other costs and the disruption likely to be caused

- the extent of the financial resources of the employer

- the availability of assistance to make adjustment

National Disability Council

This advises the Government on relevant issues, including the operation of legislation, although it does not have as many powers as the Equal Opportunities Commission or Commission for Racial Equality in investigating or supporting individual's complaints.

Harassment

Racial and sexual harassment have been held to be unlawful direct discrimination by the RRA and the SDA, even though neither are defined as distinct offences under those Acts.

There is an increased awareness of the issues involved in racial and sexual harassment, and recent years have shown a significant rise in complaints to employment tribunals. If the complaint is serious, employment tribunals will award high damages. Therefore, it is crucial for employers to take steps to prevent harassment occurring in their work place. Where it does occur they should deal with it appropriately.

Definition

DEFINITION

Although there is no legal definition of racial and sexual harassment it is accepted that behaviour that falls within the scope is quite varied, including physical, verbal and non-verbal conduct. The conduct must be unwanted by the recipient and used, to the recipient's detriment, as a basis for employment decisions.

More detailed guidance can be found in the European Commission's recommendation and code of practice *Protection of the Dignity of Men and Women at Work* in relation to sexual harassment and the CRE's *Racial Harassment At Work* in relation to racial harassment.

Employer responsibility for harassment

Racial and sexual harassment fall under discrimination legislation and therefore the employer is liable for the acts of its employees in the course of their employment. It is not always clear whether an act of harassment should be regarded as 'in the course of employment'. If the harasser is acting in a supervisory role, his or her act of harassment is more likely to be deemed to be in the course of employment than if the harasser is in a subordinate position.

Employers, however, can avoid liability for the action of an employee in the course of employment if they can prove that they took such steps as were reasonably practicable to prevent the employee from committing a certain act, or from committing acts of that description in the course of his or her employment. This defence has been examined earlier in this chapter.

Preventing harassment

The best way to avoid racial and sexual harassment complaints is to ensure that harassment does not occur in the first place. Employers should have an equal opportunities policy and a sexual and racial harassment policy which define harassment and state that it should not occur (see model equal opportunities policy at end of chapter 2). Employees must be made aware of the existence of these policies, educated about harassment and warned of its consequences.

Employees should be aware that acts of harassment are taken very seriously by the employer and will be considered gross misconduct.

Dealing with harassment complaints

Complaints of harassment can be very disruptive to the work place and must be dealt with very carefully. If an employee complains of harassment, consider whether an informal approach to the harasser would be appropriate, i.e. if it is a less serious complaint or the first instance of harassment. Consider whether the person complaining of harassment wants an informal approach or would rather more formal action be taken.

If an informal warning is appropriate, the alleged harasser should be consulted to explain that the conduct is upsetting the employee, and that it is considered harassment and must not continue. He or she should also be warned that the matter will be kept under review. He or she must be shown the policy which is in place and warned that if matters do not improve disciplinary action will be taken. The person who has complained of harassment should be kept informed of the warning given and told to inform the employer if he or she has any further complaints against the alleged harasser.

Where an informal approach is inappropriate or if the complainant wants formal action taken, the disciplinary procedure should be followed in the following way:

- Ask the complainant for a full statement.

- Suspend the alleged harasser pending the investigation of the complaint (if appropriate).

- Take statements from all staff who can provide evidence about the alleged harassment.

- Interview the alleged harasser and invite him or her to provide a statement. A disciplinary hearing to give the alleged harasser the opportunity to answer the complaint or justify or excuse his or her conduct will be necessary if there is substance to or doubt in relation to the matters complained of.

- Very often there will be no witnesses and it will be one word against the other, leaving it to the employer to decide which version to believe.

- If the conclusion is that harassment has taken place consider a penalty. In serious cases the likely outcome will be dismissal although, in some circumstances, it may be appropriate to transfer the harasser. With harassment of a less serious nature, a final written warning will be appropriate.

Criminal Justice & Public Order Act 1994

Under this Act, there is now a criminal offence of intentional harassment, alarm or distress which renders racial, sexual and all other forms of harassment including harassment against homosexuals and disabled persons at work and in the street a criminal offence punishable by six months' imprisonment or a fine of £5,000. It is necessary to prove that the harasser's action was intentional and also that someone was actually harassed.

This offence relates to harassment by an individual and is of little use in the employment context, although employers may be under a duty to inform employees of their rights under the Act.

Protection from Harassment Act 1997

Under this Act, is is now an offence for someone to pursue a course of conduct which amounts to harassment of another and which he or she knows, or ought to know, amounts to harassment. In addition to providing for harassers to be subject potentially to a fine of up to six months' imprisonment, the Act creates a number of civil remedies including damages and restraining order backed by powers of arrest.

Termination of employment

Chapter 5

Termination of employment

All employers must at some time deal with the termination of contracts of employment. Many employers associate termination of employment with the anxiety and expense of proceedings being brought against them by a disgruntled employee. This does not have to be the case if the employer is aware of the contractual and statutory duties in relation to termination so that termination can be effected in a legally acceptable way.

This chapter describes the various ways contracts of employment can be brought to an end, the potential problems that can arise and the recommended procedure for avoiding such problems.

DEFINITION

Dismissal

In the context of termination of employment, 'dismissal' is defined as occurring in the following situations, each of which is discussed in subsequent sections:

(a) the employee's contract of employment is terminated by the employer with or without notice;

(b) the employee works under a fixed-term contract and the term expires without renewal under the same contract;

(c) the employee terminates his or her own contract, with or without notice, in circumstances such that he or she is entitled to by reason of the employer's conduct. This is known as 'constructive dismissal' (see page 122).

DEFINITION

'Unfair dismissal' arises from statutory rights (see page 127 for details) whereas 'wrongful dismissal' arises from contractual rights (see page 132 for details).

(a) Termination by employer with or without notice

Termination with notice

The proper notice to be given is often specified in the contract of employment; the written statement given to the employee must include the length of notice which the employee is obliged to give and entitled to receive (see page 27). However, if a notice period has not been expressly agreed, there is an implied term that it may be terminated upon reasonable notice. Just what is reasonable notice will depend on the case in question, taking into account the seniority, age, length of service, remuneration of the employee and what is usual in the industry.

Whatever the contractual provisions for termination of the contract, the notice actually given must not be less than the statutory minimum period of notice (see page 27). If proper notice is given there can be no claim for wrongful dismissal. However, there may still be a valid claim for unfair dismissal if proper notice is given. Conversely, a dismissal may be fair even though proper notice is not given.

Pay in lieu of notice

It is common for an employer terminating an employment contract to want the employee to cease working immediately. This is because very often an employee who knows he or she is leaving will not carry out his or her work effectively and can be disruptive in the work place. In these circumstances it is usual for the employer to pay the employee a sum in lieu of notice or compensation for failure to give notice.

Sometimes the contract will provide that it may be terminated either by notice, or without notice on payment of a sum in lieu. In these circumstances the employee is entitled to the pay in lieu under a contractual obligation on the employer to make the payment, and tax and National Insurance deductions should be made in the usual way.

Usually however, there is nothing in a contract relating to making payments in lieu. In these circumstances payment may be considered as compensation for the employer's breach of contract in not giving notice and in some circumstances may be paid tax-free up to a limit of £30,000. But, it is not always entirely clear whether payment should be seen as compensation or as payment in lieu of notice so it is worth seeking advice on this point.

When compensation is being paid free of tax, the fact that it is compensation should be stated to the employee in writing, with a condition that the employee agrees to reimburse the employer in the event that it becomes liable to pay tax in relation to the payment. See the example letter 12 from an employer dismissing with payment in lieu of notice. If there is any doubt about whether or not the sum should be paid tax-free, clearance can be sought from the Inland Revenue in advance.

Compensation must be assessed to put the employee in the same position, with respect to damages for the employer's breach of contract of employment, as if the contract had been performed during the notice period. Therefore, it is not only the employee's salary but also all benefits, such as company car, that must be included in the calculation.

Termination without notice

Dismissal without notice is a breach of contract by the employer rendering him or her liable in damages for wrongful dismissal (see page 132). The exception is when the employee has acted in gross misconduct in which case the employer is justified in dismissing with immediate effect. A contract often expresses the right of the employer to dismiss the employee without notice; but in any event the employer should give its employees a clear indication of what type of conduct it regards as gross misconduct. This will depend upon the type of employment in question, as conduct which constitutes gross misconduct in one area of employment might not be considered to be so serious in another. Examples may be included in the disciplinary procedure, although it should be made clear that the examples given are not exhaustive. Examples of gross misconduct are: theft, damage to the employer's property, incapacity for work due to being under the influence of alcohol or illegal drugs, physical assault and gross insubordination.

(b)   **Expiry of a fixed-term contract**

A fixed-term contract will automatically terminate at the end of the term, without any notice having to be given. However, if a fixed-term contract is not renewed the employee may have a valid claim for redundancy pay or in respect of unfair dismissal. The exception to this is if the employee has agreed to exclude his or her statutory redundancy payment rights (see pages 39-40). This right to require an employee to exclude his or her statutory redundancy rights is due to be abolished in October 2002.

A fixed-term contract can be extended where an employee remains in the employment after the expiry of the term. In these circumstances, contract of employment will continue with an implied term that it may be terminated by either party giving reasonable notice.

(c)   **Constructive dismissal**

If the employer's conduct is such that it is in fundamental breach of the contract of employment, the employee may resign with immediate effect. In such circumstances the employee may have a valid claim for unfair dismissal and for wrongful dismissal.

Resigned or constructively dismissed?

Where an employee complains of unfair and constructive dismissal, it is common for the employer to argue that the employee resigned and dismissal did not occur. The employee would have to prove that the employer's conduct clearly breached and repudiated the contract entitling him or her to leave without notice (whether he or she gave notice or not).

The employee must have considered that the contract was at an end because of the employer's conduct. The employer's conduct is sufficient to justify the employee leaving and complaining of constructive dismissal if it:

- was a significant breach going to the root of the contract of employment; or

- showed that the employer no longer intended to be bound by one or more of the essential terms of the contract.

Very often constructive dismissal occurs as a result of a breach of the implied terms of trust and confidence in the contract (i.e. a breakdown in the employment relationship). This can be caused by a single action by the employer (such as verbal abuse) or by a series of less serious actions which together amount to a breach of the terms.

If an employer makes a statement of clear intention to breach an essential term of the contract, the employee can leave and claim constructive dismissal based on an anticipatory breach of the contract.

The employee must leave quickly because of the breach of contract. If he or she does not leave soon after the incident or incidents complained of the employer can argue that the employee accepted the alleged breach and therefore, no constructive dismissal will have occurred.

Other terminations

Resignation

Resignation by an employee should be with notice. The period of notice to be given by an employee is subject to a statutory minimum of one week, although the contractual notice period will in many cases be longer. The contractual notice period may be either expressly agreed upon or implied. If implied, the notice period must be considered a reasonable period under all the circumstances.

An employee is entitled to continue to receive all benefits for the notice period provided he or she is ready and willing to work for that period. However, the parties may agree that the employee may stop working before the end of the full notice period.

An employer is advised to ensure that clear words of resignation are used. Words spoken in the heat of the moment should not be relied upon as terminating the employment, as they may not amount to a resignation. The employment would then be deemed to be terminated by dismissal by the employer and the employee would have a right to make a claim of unfair dismissal.

The employer should accept resignation and communicate this acceptance to the employee. Once accepted the employee may not withdraw the resignation without the employer's consent.

It is a good idea to ask the employee why he or she is leaving. Answers may alert the employer to potential problems with other employees. A written note of the employee's reasons for leaving should be kept.

If an employee resigns without giving notice he or she will be in breach of contract unless it is in response to a fundamental breach of contract by the employer (i.e. constructive dismissal). If the employee does resign without giving notice the employer can contractually require the employee to serve out the period of notice which he or she should have given, but in practice this would be very difficult to enforce because a court may not compel an employee to work. However, the employer should not pay the employee for any time after the date of resignation. The employee is not entitled to pay in lieu of the notice.

An employer may want an employee to serve out the correct period of notice to prevent the employee from immediately joining a competitor. A better way to do this may be to include a clause in the employee's contract restraining him or her (after leaving the employment) from working for a competitor. However, such restriction must be for a reasonable period of time only, and within a reasonable geographical distance from the former employer. Such clauses have to be carefully worded as the employee must be able to continue to earn a living. Such clauses shall only be enforceable if they are reasonably required for the protection of the employer's legitimate business interests. Alternatively or in addition, an employer may include what is known as a 'garden leave' clause in the contract of employment. Garden leave describes the situation where an employee serving their notice of termination is required to remain at home although they continue to be paid. The aim behind this practice is to prevent the employee from leaving to work for a competitor while not having that employee around at work where he or she may obtain confidential information. Employers wishing to include restrictive clauses or garden leave clauses in their contracts of employment should consult a solicitor.

Redundancy

See page 133 for details.

Mutual agreement

The parties may mutually agree to terminate the contract of employment at any time. But if it is clear that the employee was forced to agree to the termination with the threat of dismissal, he or she will be held to have been unfair dismissed. Financial inducements to agree to terminate the employment are, however, fully acceptable.

If the parties mutually agree to end the contract, no notice of termination need be given by the employer. There will be no entitlement to pay in lieu of notice or redundancy pay. However it is fairly usual for the employer to make a payment described as an 'ex gratia payment' to avoid any implication of dismissal.

Retirement

If an employer requires an employee to retire at a certain age, this should be included in the contract of employment. An employee may continue in employment beyond pensionable age for as long as he is able to work, unless there is an agreed upon retirement date or there is a recognised customary date for retirement in the trade or industry.

The right to complain of unfair dismissal and to claim a redundancy payment ceases when an employee reaches the normal retiring age of his or her employer or, if there is no normal retiring age, at the age of 65.

Death

Unless a contract of employment provides otherwise, the death of either party terminates the contract.

Frustration

DEFINITION

'Frustration' of a contract of employment occurs when some outside event happens that is not the fault of either party to the contract. The outside event must have been unforeseen by the parties when they entered into the contract and it must make it impossible for the contract to be performed at all, or it must make its performance radically different from its original purpose. If frustration occurs, the contract is terminated automatically without any need for either party to give notice.

Examples of frustration occurring are when an employee suffers an illness and as a result can never work again. Frustration may also occur if the employee is sentenced to prison.

In unfair dismissal cases employers have argued that there has been no dismissal but termination by frustration instead. It is not advisable to rely on frustration to avoid an unfair dismissal complaint, as employment tribunals do not readily accept that a contract has been terminated by frustration.

Insolvency of the employer

An employer's insolvency has the effect of terminating the contract of employment.

The employees may apply to the employer's representative for payment and if payment is not forthcoming, they may make an application to the Secretary of State for payment.

Claims and settlements for termination

In the preceding sections of this chapter reference has been made to claims of unfair dismissal, wrongful dismissal and redundancy payments. These are explored in further detail below to give employers an idea of potential liabilities and recommendations on how they might resolve these disputes.

Claims

(a) **Unfair dismissal**

note

Dismissal of an employee without good reason, or without following a fair procedure, is likely to be unfair, liable to an unfair dismissal claim in an employment tribunal. The right not to be unfairly dismissed is a statutory right effective when the employment contract is entered into. It is subject to certain qualifying conditions.

Qualifying conditions

note

To bring a claim for unfair dismissal, an employee must currently have been employed under a contract for a minimum continuous period of one year from the commencement of the contract until the effective date of termination, and he or she must have been dismissed. In addition he or she must not be over normal retirement age or, if there is no retirement age, 65.

Continuity of employment remains unbroken even if there has been a transfer of business ownership, or employee absence from work because of sickness, injury, pregnancy or confinement (rules for assessing what is continuous employment are set out in sections 210–219 of the Employment Rights Act 1996).

The effective date of termination is either the date notice to terminate expires, the date of termination of employment or, if a fixed-term contract, the date on which it expires unrenewed. If the employer has not given the statutory minimum period of notice (except when entitled to dismiss without notice) the effective date of termination is the date when the statutory minimum period of notice to which the employee is entitled expires.

The time limit for bringing a claim for unfair dismissal is three months from the effective date of termination of the contract. An employment tribunal will extend the time limit when it is not practicable to bring the claim within this limit.

No qualifying period of service is required if the dismissal is for any of the following reasons:

- membership or non-membership of an independent trade union or taking part in activities of an independent trade union;

- a maternity-related reason;

- a health and safety reason;

- asserting statutory rights;

- performance by an employee representative (or candidate to be an employee representative);

- the performance by an employee who is a pension scheme trustee.

- a shop or betting worker for refusing to work on a Sunday;

- a reason connected with the Working Time Regulations;

- a reason related to making protected disclosure (i.e. 'whistle-blowing');

- a reason related to securing the benefit of the national minimum wage; or

- for enforcing a right to working family tax credits; or

- taking part in 'protected' industrial action.

An employee who is dismissed on medical grounds specified in any health and safety at work law, regulation or code of practice can make a claim for unfair dismissal provided he or she has one month's continuous employment.

No contracting-out

Employers cannot exclude or waive an employee's right not to be unfairly dismissed. The inclusion of such a term in a contract of employment would have no legal effect, leaving the employee at liberty to bring a complaint of unfair dismissal in the employment tribunal.

There are exceptions to this principle, and an agreement that limits the right not to be unfairly dismissed is effective in the following circumstances:

- if the agreement is reached through a conciliation officer from ACAS (see page 135);

- if it is a valid compromise agreement (see page 135);

Reasons for dismissal

If an employee can prove that he or she has all the qualifying conditions to bring a claim for unfair dismissal, the employer then has to establish the reason, or principal reason (if there was more than one), for the dismissal and prove it falls within one of the following acceptable reasons:

- connected to the capability or qualifications of the employee for performing work of the kind which he or she was employed to do; capability is assessed by reference to skill, aptitude, health or any other physical or mental quality (example letters 10 and 11 are examples of dismissal letters for capability and sickness – where dismissal is for one of the other reasons, these letters can be adapted accordingly);

- connected to the conduct of the employee; or

- redundancy; or

- the employee could not continue to work in the position which he or she held without violating (either on his or her part or on that of his or her employer) a duty or restriction imposed by or under a law; or

- connected with some other substantial reason of a kind sufficient to justify the dismissal of an employee.

If the employer can satisfy the employment tribunal that the reason or principal reason for dismissal is one of the above, the tribunal will consider whether dismissal was fair or unfair. The tribunal will look at the reason given by the employer, all the circumstances surrounding the dismissal including the size and administrative resources of the employer, in order to decide the reasonableness of the dismissal. If the employment tribunal is not satisfied that dismissal was for an acceptable reason, dismissal shall be ruled unfair.

Test of reasonableness

The decisive factor at this stage is whether or not the employer followed a fair procedure, appropriate in the circumstances, leading up to the dismissal. This is why the practice of using standard, fair procedures for the various circumstances that arise during the employment relationship can be crucial to avoid liability for unfair dismissal. Different procedures are appropriate for the different circumstances. This Guide includes various procedure flowcharts at the end of this chapter for reference (see page 137).

Automatically unfair dismissals

Dismissal for any of the following reasons is automatically unfair:

- membership or non-membership of an independent trade union or taking part in activities of an independent trade union

- a maternity-related reason (see pages 79-80)

- a health and safety reason

- asserting statutory rights

- performance by an employee representative (or candidate to be an employee representative)

- performance by an employee who is a pension scheme trustee

- on the transfer of an undertaking i.e. where the ownership of the employer is transferred from one person/entity to another

- a spent conviction or failure to disclose a spent conviction

- unfair selection for redundancy i.e. selection will be unfair if it is for any of the above reasons

- taking parental leave or taking time off for dependants, and performing functions as an employee representative (or as a candidate to be an employee representative) for the purposes of establishing a workforce agreement in relation to parental leave

- making a protected disclosure (whistleblowing)

- a national minimum wage reason

- for enforcing a right to working family tax credit, or

- taking part in protected industrial action.

Note that it is only necessary for the employee to establish a period of continuous employment in the last two above situations.

Remedies

If a tribunal finds that dismissal has been unfair it may make an order for reinstatement (for the employee to return to his or her original job), re-engagement (for the employee to be placed in employment comparable to that from which he or she was dismissed or other suitable employment) or compensation (up to a statutory maximum limit).

Compensation is the most common remedy and usually comprises a basic award and a compensatory award. Further details of these are set out below. In addition, there are further awards made in certain circumstances, such as an 'additional award' if the employer fails to comply with an order for reinstatement or re-engagement, and a 'special award' if the employer fails to comply with an order for reinstatement or re-engagement where dismissal was on the grounds of trade union membership or activities or health and safety duties.

(i)   Basic award

The basic award is calculated by considering the employee's age, length of continuous service and gross average weekly wage. Each completed year of service up to a maximum of 20 counts for payment on the following scale (with a maximum of £250 for a week's pay):

- up to 22 years of age – $1/2$ week's pay;

- between 22 and up to 41 years of age – 1 week's pay;

- between 41 and up to 65 years of age – $1\frac{1}{2}$ week's pay.

Where an employee is dismissed after his or her 64th birthday the basic award is reduced by one twelfth for every month after that.

The current maximum basic award is £7,500 (i.e. $1\frac{1}{2}$ x 20 x 250).

A tribunal will reduce the basic award if it considers it is just and equitable to do so.

(ii)   Compensatory award

The compensatory award is an amount the employment tribunal considers just and equitable, in all the circumstances relating to the loss sustained by the employee, as a result of the dismissal. The award is calculated on the net value of wages, other benefits and expenses reasonably incurred by the employee as a result of the dismissal.

Factors an employment tribunal will take into account to reduce the award are:

- contributory fault

- whether dismissal would have resulted even if the employer had acted reasonably

- the employee's duty to minimise his or her loss by attempting to seek other employment

- payments made by the employer

- what is just and equitable

Once the assessment of the compensatory award has been made, the statutory limit, which is currently £52,600 (except in cases of refusal to comply with a reinstatement or re-engagement order), must be applied. This statutory limit does not apply where the dismissal is as a result of making a protected disclosure (i.e. whistleblowing).

(b)   **Wrongful dismissal**

DEFINITION

Wrongful dismissal is a common law remedy distinct from unfair dismissal. It occurs when an employer terminates an employee's contract of employment in a way that breaches it or the employer's conduct is such that it entitles the employee to resign (i.e. constructive dismissal). In these circumstances the employee may take proceedings against the employer in an employment tribunal or in the civil courts (County Court or the High Court) for wrongful dismissal claiming damages for breach of contract. There is no requirement for the employee to have a qualifying period of continuous employment to make such a claim.

Damages are assessed on the basis that they should put the employee in the position he or she would have been in had the contract been performed in accordance with its terms. This is subject to a duty of the employee to mitigate his or her loss (e.g. minimising his or her loss by seeking other employment). Damages for wrongful dismissal are usually assessed by reference to the period of notice by which the employer could lawfully have terminated the contract. However, if the employee has been dismissed in breach of a contractual disciplinary procedure, the damages may be assessed with reference to the time that it would have taken to go through the disciplinary procedure.

Employees are not entitled to damages for loss, injury to feelings or distress arising from the manner of dismissal, and generally nor are they entitled to damages for injury to reputation. However, recent case law has concluded that if an employer has damaged the employee's chance of obtaining further employment through loss of reputation, he may also be liable to compensate for continuing financial loss which the employee suffers as a result.

(c) **Redundancy**

Employees in a redundancy situation are entitled to a statutory redundancy payment. Also, if dismissal by reason of redundancy is not effected in a reasonable way, it may amount to unfair dismissal.

Definition of a redundancy situation

DEFINITION

A redundancy situation exists where an employee's dismissal was attributable wholly or mainly to the fact that:

- the employer has ceased, or intends to cease, to carry on the business for which the employee was employed or has ceased, or intends to cease, to carry it on at a place where the employee was employed (i.e. relocation); or

- the business's need for work for which employees were taken on has, or is expected to, cease or diminish (i.e. reduction in the number of employees required).

Statutory redundancy payment

Employees in a redundancy situation are entitled to a statutory redundancy payment if they have at least two years' service after reaching the age of 18. The entitlement is calculated in the same way as the basic award for unfair dismissal claims (except employment prior to reaching 18 is not counted). The calculation is made by considering the employee's age, length of continuous service and gross average weekly wage. Each completed year of service, up to a maximum of 20 after the age of 18, counts for payment on the following scale (with a maximum of £250 for a week's pay):

- between 18 and up to 22 years of age – ½ week's pay;
- between 22 and up to 41 years of age – 1 week's pay;
- between 41 and up to 65 years of age – 1½ weeks' pay.

Where an employee is made redundant after his or her 64th birthday the payment is reduced by one-twelfth for every month after that.

The current maximum redundancy payment is £7,500 (i.e. 1½ x 20 x 250).

An employee may raise a complaint with an employment tribunal if he or she has not received the correct redundancy payment. The time limit for such a claim is six months from the relevant date as defined by Section 145 of the Employment Rights Act 1996 (usually the effective date of termination). The time limit may be extended for a further six months if approved by the employment tribunal.

An employee is not entitled to statutory redundancy payment if, before existing employment ends, the employer offers him or her (orally or in writing), employment on the same terms or suitable alternative employment, to commence within 4 weeks of the ending of the original employment. If the employee unreasonably refuses such an offer, or during a trial period for the new job unreasonably terminates such employment, he or she loses the right to statutory redundancy payment.

If the employee leaves employment before dismissal takes effect, and the employer objects in writing, the employment tribunal may determine the extent of the employee's entitlement.

Unfair dismissal

Dismissal for redundancy may be unfair, by a failure by the employer to comply with the obligation to consult with appropriate representatives of the employees concerned. These are either representatives of an independent trade union or other elected representatives. Failure to adhere to an agreed redundancy procedure does not render a dismissal automatically unfair, but may be relevant to the tribunal's view of the procedure actually adopted by the employer (see Flowchart 6).

The amount of a basic award will be reduced by the amount of any redundancy payment awarded by a tribunal or paid by the employer in respect of the same dismissal.

Settlements and arbitration

Where there is a dispute, the parties will often prefer to settle the matter rather than proceed to a hearing. A settlement agreement is only binding if either of the following courses are taken:

(a) **ACAS conciliation**

One way to contract out validly of an employee's right to pursue a case to a tribunal is by means of a settlement promoted by an ACAS conciliation officer. A conciliation officer has a duty to promote a settlement once a complaint has been put to a tribunal if requested to do so by the complainant, the employee concerned, or if in the absence of such request, the conciliation officer considers there is a reasonable prospect of achieving a settlement.

Settlements are recorded on ACAS form COT 3, signed by the parties and contain a clause under which the complainant agrees that no further proceedings arising out of the matter will be pursued by him or her.

(b) **Compromise agreements**

The only other way to settle a matter validly is by making a compromise agreement between the parties, in full and final settlement.

For a compromise agreement to be effective, it must be in writing and must fulfil the following conditions:

- it must relate to the particular complaint;

- the employee must have received independent legal advice from a qualified lawyer, an officer of an independent trade union or a worker at an advice centre as to the terms and effect of the proposed agreement, and in particular its effects on his or her ability to pursue the appropriate rights before an employment tribunal. The advisor who gives the advice must have an insurance policy covering the risk of a claim by the employee for an alleged loss arising out of the advice;

- the agreement must identify the advisor;

- the agreement must declare that the above conditions are satisfied.

If none of these courses is taken the employee shall still be at liberty to commence proceedings despite the fact that he or she has received a compensation payment to settle. If he or she does proceed to make a claim however, the payment can be taken into account when assessing compensation.

However, if the dispute is only in relation to wrongful dismissal, (i.e. it is only a contractual claim), the parties may settle validly by agreement without the need for any special requirements to be satisfied. You will find basic example compromise agreements for unfair dismissal and redundancy at the end of this chapter.

(c)   **ACAS Arbitration Scheme**

This scheme gives parties to straightforward claims of unfair dismissal the option of having an independent arbitrator rule on the case, whose decision is final and binding and there is no right of appeal (except in very limited circumstances).

Flowchart 1
Capability procedures
(for responding to an employee's poor performance)

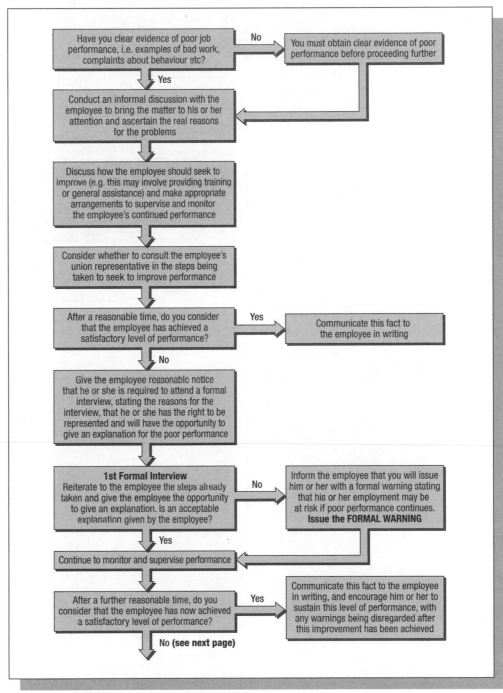

Flowchart 1 (continued)
Capability procedures
(for responding to an employee's poor performance) (continued)

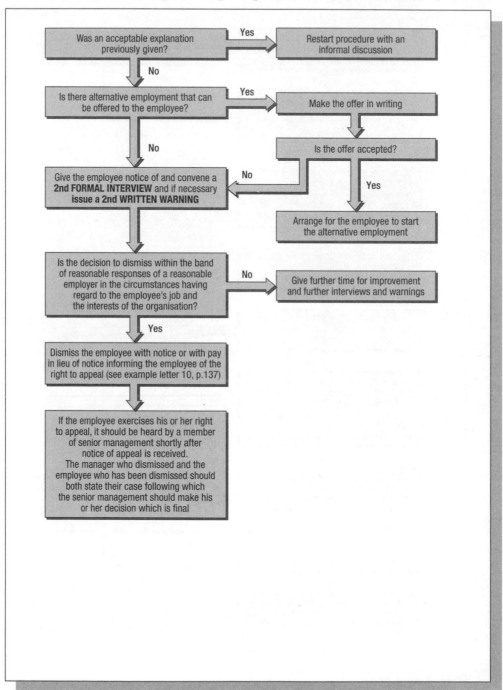

Flowchart 2
Sickness procedures
(for responding to an employee's prolonged absence or frequent short absences)

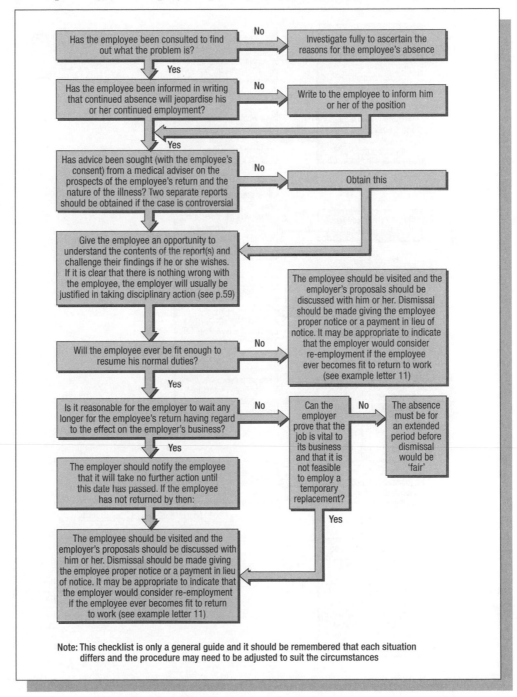

Has the employee been consulted to find out what the problem is? — **No** → Investigate fully to ascertain the reasons for the employee's absence

↓ **Yes**

Has the employee been informed in writing that continued absence will jeopardise his or her continued employment? — **No** → Write to the employee to inform him or her of the position

↓ **Yes**

Has advice been sought (with the employee's consent) from a medical adviser on the prospects of the employee's return and the nature of the illness? Two separate reports should be obtained if the case is controversial — **No** → Obtain this

↓

Give the employee an opportunity to understand the contents of the report(s) and challenge their findings if he or she wishes. If it is clear that there is nothing wrong with the employee, the employer will usually be justified in taking disciplinary action (see p.59)

↓

Will the employee ever be fit enough to resume his normal duties? — **No** → The employee should be visited and the employer's proposals should be discussed with him or her. Dismissal should be made giving the employee proper notice or a payment in lieu of notice. It may be appropriate to indicate that the employer would consider re-employment if the employee ever becomes fit to return to work (see example letter 11)

↓ **Yes**

Is it reasonable for the employer to wait any longer for the employee's return having regard to the effect on the employer's business? — **No** → Can the employer prove that the job is vital to its business and that it is not feasible to employ a temporary replacement? — **No** → The absence must be for an extended period before dismissal would be 'fair'

↓ **Yes**   ↓ **Yes**

The employer should notify the employee that it will take no further action until this date has passed. If the employee has not returned by then:

↓

The employee should be visited and the employer's proposals should be discussed with him or her. Dismissal should be made giving the employee proper notice or a payment in lieu of notice. It may be appropriate to indicate that the employer would consider re-employment if the employee ever becomes fit to return to work (see example letter 11)

Note: This checklist is only a general guide and it should be remembered that each situation differs and the procedure may need to be adjusted to suit the circumstances

Flowchart 3
Procedure for dealing with lack of qualifications

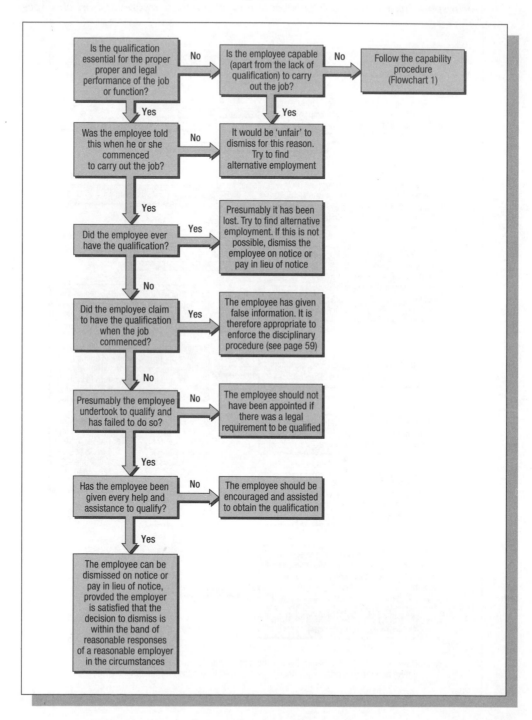

Flowchart 4
Misconduct procedures
(for breach of the Employer's Disciplinary Rules)

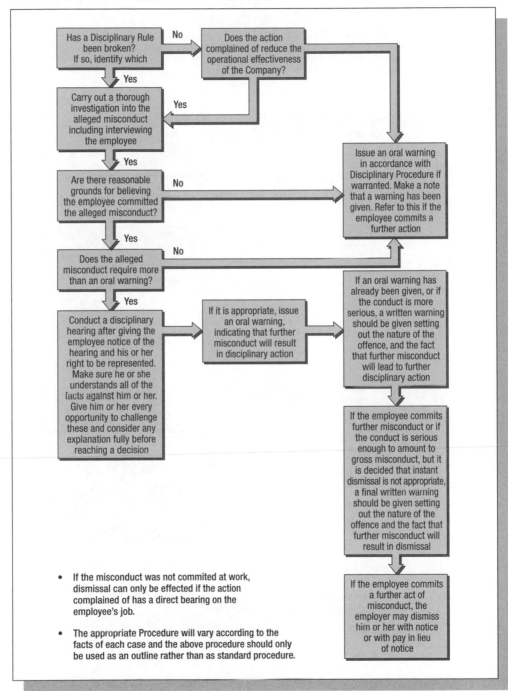

Flowchart 5

Gross misconduct procedures
(for responding to conduct warranting instant dismissal)

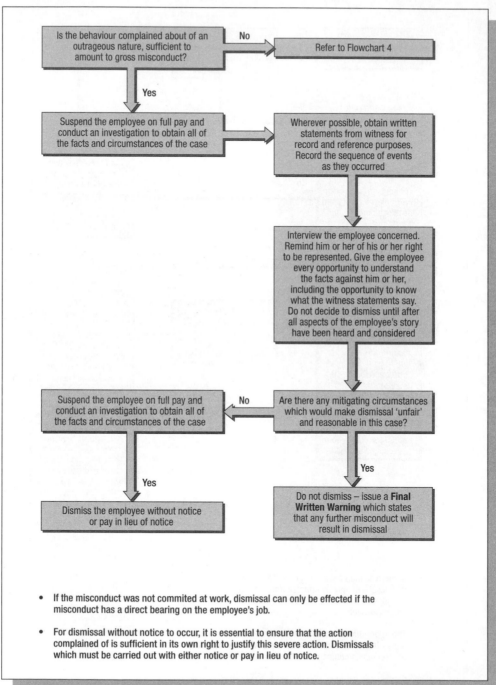

- If the misconduct was not commited at work, dismissal can only be effected if the misconduct has a direct bearing on the employee's job.

- For dismissal without notice to occur, it is essential to ensure that the action complained of is sufficient in its own right to justify this severe action. Dismissals which must be carried out with either notice or pay in lieu of notice.

Flowchart 6
Redundancy procedure

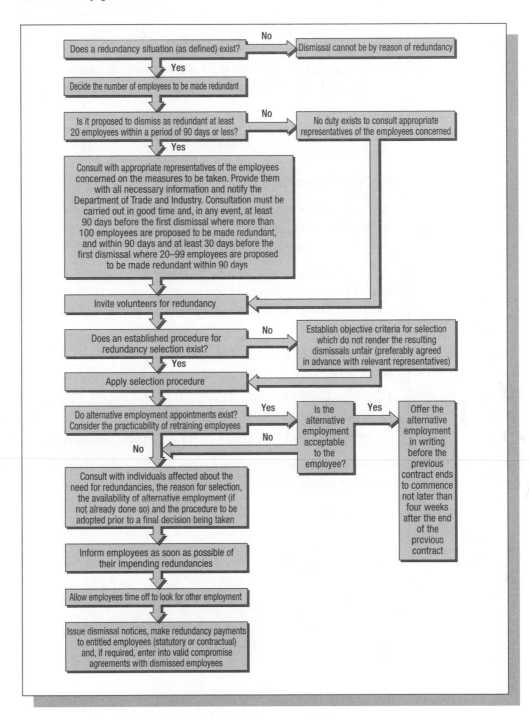

Example Letter 10
Notice of dismissal (capability)

Ace Fabrics Limited

16 Willow Walk, Retford, Nottingham NG6 8WS
Tel: (01777) 121211 Fax: (01777) 121233 Email: acf@uk

Dear *Miss Porter*,

I refer to our meeting on *15 July 2002*.

As I explained at the meeting, you have been unable to carry out your duties to the standards required by the Company. Therefore, we have no alternative but to terminate your employment with the Company with effect from *15 August 2002*.

As you are aware, we have provided you with training and assistance to enable you to improve your performance but without success. In addition, we have attempted to find suitable alternative employment within the Company, but regret that nothing is available.

You are entitled to be paid in full, including any accrued holiday pay, during your notice period.

I take this opportunity of reminding you that you are entitled to appeal against this decision through the Company's disciplinary procedure. If you wish to exercise this right you must let me know within two working days of receipt of this letter.

It is with regret that we have had to take this action. We should like to thank you for your past efforts for the Company and wish you every success for the future.

Yours sincerely

John Smith

John Smith
Personnel Manager

Registered Office: 16 Willow Walk, Retford, Nottingham NG6 8WS
Reg. No: England 1212298762

1 This letter is an example of dismissal due to terminal illness. Such a letter would have to be re-worded if the employee was likely to be able to resume work at some future date.

Example Letter 11
Notice of dismissal (sickness)[1]

Ace Fabrics Limited

16 Willow Walk, Retford, Nottingham NG6 8WS
Tel: (01777) 121211 Fax: (01777) 121233 Email: acf@uk

Dear *Miss Porter,*

I refer to our meeting at your home on *18 July 2002.*

I was very sorry to hear that your condition has not improved and that it is unlikely that you will be able to resume working.

As we discussed, there is little we can do to assist your return to work and our medical adviser has reported that you are not likely to be well enough to return to your current job for some time, if at all. We have tried to find some alternative suitable work for you but, as you know, all of the work in this Company is fairly heavy work and there is nothing we can offer you.

I regret that I have no alternative other than to give you notice to terminate your employment with the Company with effect from *22 August 2002.*

You are entitled to full pay for the period of your notice plus accrued holiday pay. I shall arrange for these sums to be paid to you, and for your P45 to be sent to you as soon as possible.

If your health does improve in the future to enable you to resume working, I would be pleased to discuss re-employing you.

Yours sincerely

John Smith

John Smith
Personnel Manager

Registered Office: 16 Willow Walk, Retford, Nottingham NG6 8WS
Reg. No: England 1212298762

Example Letter 12
Notice of redundancy

Ace Fabrics Limited

16 Willow Walk, Retford, Nottingham NG6 8WS
Tel: (01777) 121211 Fax: (01777) 121233 Email: acf@uk

Dear *Miss Porter,*

It is with regret that I write to inform you that the Company had decided to make you redundant with effect from today. You are aware that the Company is being restructured and the volume of work has substantially diminished.

We have tried to find you a suitable position commensurate with your abilities elsewhere within the Company but there is nothing available.

You are entitled to *one month's* notice of termination but we believe it is better for you and all others concerned if you leave immediately. The Company will pay you a gross sum of *£1,223.39* as compensation for the termination of your employment subject to such deductions as the Company is required to make from the sum in respect of any tax charges or levies. This sum is calculated as follows:

(a)	*4 weeks' gross salary at £13,500 per annum*	*£1,038.46*
(b)	*5 days* accrued holiday	*£184.93*

In addition, the Company will make you a statutory redundancy payment of *£1,125*. This is calculated in accordance with your age, salary (subject to a statutory maximum of £250 per week) and the number of years service with the Company.

> i.e. *1½ x £250 x 3*

1. The Company will therefore pay you a total sum of *£2,348.39* immediately on your signature and return of the enclosed copy of this letter.

continued...

Registered Office: 16 Willow Walk, Retford, Nottingham NG6 8WS
Reg. No: England 1212298762

1 A compromise agreement is needed to refrain the employee from bringing proceedings in an employment tribunal.

Example Letter 12
Notice of redundancy (continued)

… (continued)

2.   You accept that this payment made by the Company is in full and final settlement of your claim for compensation and/or damages for the termination of your employment with effect from today.[1]

3.   You will return all property in your possession belonging to the Company.

Please acknowledge receipt of this letter by signing and returning the acknowledgement on the enclosed copy of this letter.

Yours sincerely

John Smith

John Smith
Personnel Manager

I acknowledge receipt of the letter of which the above is a copy and of the compensation payment referred to in it.

Signed ....

Date of Signature

Model compromise agreement
Unfair dismissal

Ace Fabrics Limited

16 Willow Walk, Retford, Nottingham NG6 8WS
Tel: (01777) 121211 Fax: (01777) 121233 Email: acf@uk

Dear *Miss Porter,*

I hereby confirm the terms we have agreed in relation to the termination of your employment with *Ace Fabrics Limited* ("the Company") with effect from *26 July 2002.*

1.   The Company will pay you without admission of any liability whatso-ever the sum of *£2,000* payable immediately on your return of the enclosed copy of this letter as compensation in respect of the claims referred to in paragraph 2 of this letter.

2.   You assert that you may have claims (and therefore could bring pro-ceedings) against the Company for any of the following claims. However, you agree to refrain from initiating any proceedings before an Employment Tribunal alleging that the Company dismissed you unfairly, discriminated against you on the grounds of race, sex or dis-ability or has made an unlawful deduction from your wages and to withdraw any such proceedings now in progress.[1]

3.   You accept that this payment made by the Company is in full and final settlement of all of the claims referred to in paragraph 2 of this letter and all claims of any kind which you may be entitled to make against the Company, its officers, shareholders or employees in connection with your employment or its termination, including any claims which are now proceeding before an Employment Tribunal.

4.   You will return all property in your possession belonging to the Company on or before *1 August 2002.*

continued...

Registered Office: 16 Willow Walk, Retford, Nottingham NG6 8WS
Reg. No: England 1212298762

2 Delete irrelevant Acts, as appropriate

Model compromise agreement
Unfair dismissal (continued)

… (continued)

5. You agree to pay any tax due in respect of the sums referred to above or to reimburse the Company for any tax the Company is required to pay in respect of such sums.

6. You agree to keep the terms of this agreement confidential.

7. We hereby state that, the conditions regulating this Agreement under Section 203 of the Employment Rights Act 1996, under Section 77 of the Sex Discrimination Act 1975, under Section 72 of the Race Relations Act 1996 and under Section 9 of the Disability Discrimination Act 1995 [2] are satisfied. You, in turn, acknowledge and understand that you are required to take independent legal advice from a qualified lawyer on the terms and effect of this agreement. The qualified lawyer who provides you with independent legal advice is required to sign the acknowledgement on the enclosed copy of this letter.

Please signify your acceptance of the above by signing and returning the acknowledgement on the enclosed copy of this letter.

Yours sincerely

John Smith

John Smith
Personnel Manager

1 The Employment Rights (Dispute Resolution) Act 1998 increases the number of people qualified to give relevant independent advice for the purposes of concluding valid compromise agreements. In addition to qualified lawyers, officers (or officials, employees or members) of an independent trade union and workers at advice centres (such as Citizens Advice Bureaux) can now sign compromise agreements. However they must still be covered by a policy of insurance or an indemnity against negligent advice provided by a professional body. If this occurs the letter should be amended accordingly.

Model compromise agreement
Unfair dismissal (acknowledgement)

Acknowledgement

I acknowledge receipt of the letter of which the above is a copy and of the sum of *£2,000* referred to in it.

I confirm that I have taken independent advice from *John Black of Black & Brown Solicitor of 2 High Street, Maidenhead, Berkshire* and I confirm and agree to the terms set out in the letter.

Signed ....

Date of Signature:

I *John Black* of *Black & Brown Solicitors* confirm that *Miss Porter* has received independent legal advice within the meaning of Section 203(4) of the Employment Rights Act 1996 as to the terms and effect of this terms of the letter of which the above is a copy and in particular its effect on her ability to pursue her rights before an employment tribunal. I also confirm that I have advised *Miss Porter* in respect of all claims and prospective proceedings that she has or may have against the company (as defined in paragraph 3 of this letter) arising out of or in connection with her employment or its termination ***EITHER*** [I am, and was at the time I gave the advice referred to, a Solicitor of the Supreme Court, holding a current practising certificate and there is, and was at the time I gave the advice, in force a policy of insurance covering the risk of a claim by *Miss Porter* in respect of any loss arising in consequence of the advice I gave] ***OR*** [I confirm that I am competent to give this advice and am authorised to do so by *(insert Trade Union/advice centre)*. I further confirm that there is in force a policy of insurance which covers the risk of a claim by *Miss Porter* in respect of any loss arising in consequence of the advice I give.[1]

Signed ....

1 It is necessary to relate to the particular proceedings or claims that the individual may have and this paragraph will therefore need to be amended on a case by case basis.

Model compromise agreement
Redundancy

Ace Fabrics Limited

16 Willow Walk, Retford, Nottingham NG6 8WS
Tel: (01777) 121211 Fax: (01777) 121233

Dear *Miss Porter,*

It is with regret that I write to inform you that the Company has decided to make you redundant with effect from *26 July 2002.* You are aware of and we have discussed the reasons for your redundancy.

We have tried to find you a suitable position commensurate with your abilities elsewhere within the Company but there is nothing available.

The Company has however decided to make you an ex gratia payment of *£2,000* as compensation for the termination of your employment. In addition, the Company will make you a statutory redundancy payment of *£1,125.*

The statutory redundancy payment is calculated in accordance with your age, salary (subject to a statutory maximum of £250 per week) and the number of years service with the Company.

i.e. $1\frac{1}{2}$ x £250 x 3

1.	The Company will therefore pay you without admission of any liability whatsoever a total sum of *£3,125* payable immediately on your return of the enclosed copy of this letter as compensation in respect of the claims referred to in paragraph 2 of this letter.

2.	You assert that you may have claims (and therefore could bring proceedings) against the Company for any of the following claims. However, you agree to refrain from initiating any proceedings before an Employment Tribunal alleging that the Company has dismissed you unfairly, discriminated against you on the grounds of race, sex or disability or has made an unlawful deduction from your wages, and to withdraw any such proceedings now in progress.[1]

continued...

Registered Office: 16 Willow Walk, Retford, Nottingham NG6 8WS
Tel: (01777) 121211 Fax: (01777) 121233
Reg. No: England 1212298762

2 Delete irrelevant Acts, as appropriate

Model compromise agreement
Redundancy (continued)

… (continued)

3.   You accept that this payment made by the Company is in full and final settlement of all of the claims referred to in paragraph 2 of this letter and all claims of any kind which you may be entitled to make against the Company, its officers, shareholders or employees in connection with your employment or its termination including any claims which are now proceeding before an Employment Tribunal.

4.   You will return all property in your possession belonging to the Company on or before *1 August 2002*.

5.   You agree to pay any tax due in respect of the sums referred to above or to reimburse the Company for any tax the Company is required to pay in respect of such sums.

6.   You agree to keep the terms of this agreement confidential.

7.   We hereby state that, the conditions regulating this Agreement under Section 203 of the Employment Rights Act 1996, under Section 77 of the Sex Discrimination Act 1975, under Section 72 of the Race Relations Act 1996 and under Section 9 of the Disability Discrimination Act 1995 [2] are satisfied. You, in turn, acknowledge and understand that you are required to take independent legal advice from a qualified lawyer on the terms and effect of this agreement. The qualified lawyer who provides you with independent legal advice is required to sign the acknowledgement on the enclosed copy of this letter.

Please signify your acceptance of the above by signing and returning the acknowledgement on the enclosed copy of this letter.

Yours sincerely

John Smith

John Smith
Personnel Manager

1 The Employment Rights
(Dispute Resolution) Act
1998 increases the number
of people qualified to give
relevant independent advice
for the purposes of
concluding valid
compromise agreements. In
addition to qualified lawyers,
officers (or officials,
employees or members) of
an independent trade union
and workers at advice
centres (such as Citizens
Advice Bureaux) can now
sign compromise
agreements. However they
must still be covered by a
policy of insurance or an
indemnity against negligent
advice provided by a
professional body. If this
occurs the letter should be
amended accordingly.

Model compromise agreement
Redundancy (acknowledgement)

Acknowledgement

I acknowledge receipt of the letter of which the above is a copy and of the sum of *£3,125* referred to in it.

I confirm that I have taken independent advice from *John Black of Black & Brown Solicitor of 2 High Street, Maidenhead, Berkshire* and I confirm and agree to the terms set out in the letter.

Signed ....

Date of Signature:

I *John Black* of *Black & Brown Solicitors* confirm that *Miss Porter* has received independent legal advice within the meaning of Section 203(4) of the Employment Rights Act 1996 as to the terms and effect of this terms of the letter of which the above is a copy and in particular its effect on her ability to pursue her rights before an employment tribunal. I also confirm that I have advised *Miss Porter* in respect of all claims and prospective proceedings that she has or may have against the company (as defined in paragraph 3 of this letter) arising out of or in connection with her employment or its termination *EITHER* [I am, and was at the time I gave the advice referred to, a Solicitor of the Supreme Court, holding a current practising certificate and there is, and was at the time I gave the advice, in force a policy of insurance covering the risk of a claim by *Miss Porter* in respect of any loss arising in consequence of thc advice I gave] *OR* [I confirm that I am competent to give this advice and am authorised to do so by *(insert Trade Union/advice centre)*. I further confirm that there is in force a policy of insurance which covers the risk of a claim by *Miss Porter* in respect of any loss arising in consequence of the advice I give.[1]

Signed ....

Appendix

Useful addresses

Advisory Conciliation and Arbitration Service (ACAS)
Head Office
Brandon House
180 Borough High Street
London SE1 1LW

Tel: 020 7210 3000
Fax: 020 7210 3645
Website: www. acas.org.uk

Commission for Racial Equality (CRE)
Head Office
Elliot House
10-12 Allington Street
London SW1E 5EH

Tel: 020 7828 7022
Fax: 020 7630 7605
Email: info@cre.gov.uk

Data Protection Registrar
Data Protection Commissioner
Wycliffe House
Waber Lane
Wilmslow SK9 5AX

Tel: 01625 545700
Fax: 01625 535777
Website: www.dataprotection.gov.uk/
    contactus.htm

Department for Education and Employment Work Permits UK
W5 Moorfoot
Sheffield S1 4PQ

Tel: 0114 259 4074
Website: www.workpermits.gov.uk

Department for Education and Employment Overseas Labour Service
W5 Moorfoot
Sheffield S1 4PQ

Tel: 0114 259 4074

Department of Trade and Industry
1 Victoria Street
London SW1H 0ET

Tel: 020 7215 5000
Fax: 020 7222 0612
Website: www.dti.gov.uk

Employment Appeal Tribunal
Audit House
58 Victoria Embankment
London EC4Y 0DS

Tel: 020 7273 1041
Fax: 020 7273 1045
Website: www.employmentappeals.gov.uk

Equal Opportunities Commission
Overseas House   Tel: 0845 6015901
Quay Street
Manchester M3 3HN

European Commission
8 Storey's Gate   Tel: 020 7973 1992
London SW1P 3AT   Fax: 020 7973 1900
                                  Website: www.europe.org.uk

European Court of Justice
BP 96   Tel: 00 352 430 31
Plateau de Kircheergh
Luxembourg

Employment Service
St Vincent House   Tel: 020 7839 5600
30 Orange Street
London WC2H 7HT

Employment Tribunal Central Enquiries
100 Southgate Street   Tel: 08457 959775
Bury St Edmunds   Fax: 01284 766334
IP33 2AQ

Health and Safety Executive Commission
Head Office   Tel: 020 7717 6000
Rose Court   (Infoline: 0541 545 500)
2 Southwark Bridge   Website: www.hse.gov.uk
London SE1 9HS

Health and Safety Executive Books
PO Box 1999   Tel: 01787 881165
Sudbury
Suffolk CO10 6FS

National Disability Council
The Adelphi
1-11 John Adam Street
London WC2N 6HT

Race Relations Employment Advisory Service
14th Floor   Tel: 0121 244 8141/2/3
Cumberland House
200 Broad Street
Birmingham B14 1TA

Tribunals, courts and official bodies

Employment tribunals

Employment tribunals determine applications relating to employment rights, the most important of which are the rights not to be unfairly dismissed; the right to a redundancy payment; the right not to be unlawfully discriminated against on grounds of sex, race or disability in relation to employment, and rights in relation to breaches of contract. The procedure is less formal than that of a court. Cases heard in tribunals may result in awards of compensation, reinstatement or re-engagement.

Employment Appeal Tribunal (EAT)

The EAT is a division of the High Court, presided over by a High Court judge. It hears appeals from the decisions of the employment tribunals on questions of law. Appeals from the EAT are to the Court of Appeal and from there to the House of Lords.

European Court of Justice

Where the decision of a case depends upon a question of European law and the answer to the question is not clear, the tribunal or court can refer the matter to the European Court of Justice.

Advisory Conciliation and Arbitration Service (ACAS)

ACAS was established, and its activities are regulated, by UK legislation. The principal function of ACAS is to promote the improvement of industrial relations, in particular by exercising its functions in relation to the settlement of trade disputes. It provides advice to employers, employers associations, workers or trade unions on any matters concerned with the wide range of industrial relations services, including conciliation, arbitration, mediation and general and specific advice on industrial relations matters. ACAS may charge fees to those who benefit from the exercise of its functions. Fees are charged at present only for certain publications and seminars, and thus not for the key function of conciliation. ACAS also produces codes of practice and guidance on matters of industrial relations practice. Employment tribunals may take account of the provisions of such codes of practice when determining the fairness of a dismissal.

Index

ex gratia payment **125**

express terms **43**

F

family-friendly rights **75–94**

fixed-term contracts **39**, **40**
   expiry of **122**

G

garden leave **124**

gender re-assignment **97**, **104**

gross misconduct **121**

guarantee payments **28**

H

harassment **113–116**
   Criminal Justice & Public Order Act
   1994 **116**
   Protection from Harassment Act 1997
   116

Health and Safety at Work etc. Act 1974
   28, **81**

holidays **31**

homosexuals **98**

I

immigration control **10**

implied terms **43–44**

income tax **71**

infertility treatment **78**

insolvency **126**

itemised pay statements **27**

J

jury service **32**

M

maternity leave **32**, **82–86**
   ordinary **82**
   additional **84**
   right to return to work **85–86**

maternity pay period **86**

maternity rights **27**, **76–89**
   antenatal care **77–78**
   protection from dismissal and
   detrimental treatment **79**
   suspension from work **81**
   unfair dismissal **128**

minimum wage **26**

N

National Disability Council **113**

national insurance **52**, **86**

National Minimum Wage Act **26**

non-competition **45**, **124**

non-EU nationals **10**

notice of termination **27**, **39**, **120**

O

obligations
   self-employed **52**

P

parental leave **33**, **90–93**

More books available from Law Pack...

How to Make Money Online

Forget the high-profile dot com failures - there are businesses out there making money online. This guide includes what will and won't sell, how to avoid e-business mistakes, how to give website visitors the confidence to buy online, getting payments, security software and systems, digital certificates and e-signatures, selling advertising space, supplying content, and much more!

Code B604	ISBN 1 902646 76 2	PB	
250 x 199mm	160pp	£9.99	Jan 2002

Online Marketing Strategies

What are your goals for your website? Is your website marketing you, or are you marketing it? And how will your website relate to your business's overall marketing strategy? This book provides guidance on building marketing into your website, on monitoring, evaluating and improving your internet or extranet site and on coordinating online and offline marketing strategies.

Code B602	ISBN 1 902646 75 4	PB	
250 x 199mm	160pp	£9.99	Dec 2001

Secrets of Successful Websites

Some websites get it right, many get it wrong. This guide divulges what makes a successful site. It covers identifying the audience and their needs, choosing the right model for your site, choosing the right technology and ISP, getting the best help with implementation, design and branding, risk management and testing procedures.

Code B601	ISBN 1 902646 74 6	PB	
250 x 199mm	160pp	£9.99	Dec 2001

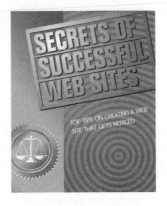

To order, visit www.lawpack.co.uk or call 020 7394 4040

More books available from Law Pack...

Legal Advice Handbook

Where do you go for legal advice? As the sources of both free and paid-for legal advice become more diverse and specific areas of law demand greater specialisation from the advice givers, the need for a consumer guide to this expanding, unmapped network has never been greater. Solicitor Tessa Shepperson has gathered together extensive research data and produced an invaluable handbook.

Code B427	ISBN 1 902646 71 1	PB	
A5	130pp	£7.99	October 2001

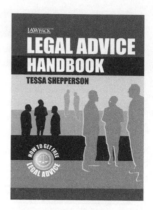

How to Complain Effectively

Faulty goods, shoddy service, poor advice... these are things most of us, at some time, feel we have good reason to complain about. In this practical guide, Steve Wiseman draws on his extensive experience as a Citizens Advice Bureau manager and tells you how to ensure your complaint has maximum impact, whether it be against your local shop or a government department.

Code B430	ISBN 1 902646 80 0	PB	
A5	160pp	£7.99	May 2001

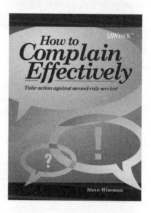

Tax Answers at a Glance

With the emphasis on self-assessment, we all need to have a hold of the panoply of taxes now levied by government. Compiled by tax experts and presented in question-and-answer format, this handy guide provides a useful summary of income tax, VAT, capital gains, inheritance, pensions, self-employment, partnerships, land and property, trusts and estates, corporation tax, stamp duty and more.

Code B425	ISBN 1 902646 62 2	PB	
A5	130pp	£7.99	April 2001

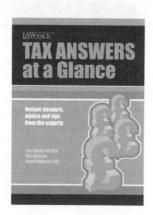

To order, visit www.lawpack.co.uk or call 020 7394 4040

More books available from Law Pack...

Company Minutes & Resolutions

Company Minutes & Resolutions Made Easy is what every busy company secretary or record-keeper needs. Maintaining good, up-to-date records is not only sensible business practice, but also a legal requirement of Companies House. This Made Easy Guide makes the whole process straightforward. It provides an invaluable source of essential documents that no company should be without.

Code B501	ISBN 1 902646 41 X	PB
250 x 199mm	190pp	£9.99	1st edition

Debt Collection

Chasing debts is a pain which all businesses can do without. Unfortunately, unpaid bills are an all-too frequent problem for business owners and managers. Debt Collection Made Easy helps you solve it. It provides expert advice and tips on resolving disputes, reducing the risks of bad debt, getting money out of reluctant payers, letter cycles, credit insurance, export credit, and much more.

Code B512	ISBN 1 902646 42 8	PB
250 x 199mm	134pp	£9.99	1st edition

Effective PR

Raise your profile with some effective PR! Nearly all businesses and organisations benefit from generating public relations activity, be it with customers or other target audiences. The author, Ian Proud, is a seasoned PR professional who tells you from the inside how to get the most out of a PR agency and also how to go about creating effective PR yourself.

Code B518	ISBN 1 902646 96 7	PB
250 x 199mm	128pp	£9.99	1st edition

To order, visit www.lawpack.co.uk or call 020 7394 4040

More books available from Law Pack...

Limited Company Formation

Incorporation as a limited liability company is the preferred structure for thousands of successful businesses. *Limited Company Formation Made Easy* Guide explains why, and shows you how to set up your own limited liability company easily and inexpensively. It provides detailed but easy to follow instructions, background information, completed examples of Companies House forms and drafts of other necessary documents.

Code B503	ISBN 1 902646 43 6	PB
250 x 199mm	112pp	£9.99	1st edition

Profitable Mail-Order

Mail-order business is big business, and it's growing year by year. Setting up and running your own mail-order business can be fun as well as profitable. This *Made Easy* Guide shows you how to do it, explaining the vital importance of product profile, building valuable mailing lists, effective advertising and a whole lot more. It divulges the mail-order secrets that ensure success!

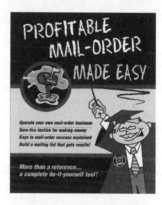

Code B510	ISBN 1 902646 46 0	PB
250 x 199mm	206pp	£9.99	1st edition

Running Your Own Business

You have a business idea that you want to put into action, but you also want advice on the realities of setting up and running a business: this *Made Easy* Guide is for you. It takes you through the business-creation process, from assessing your aptitude and ideas, to funding and business plans.

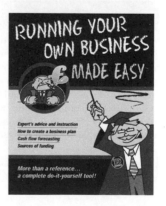

Code B511	ISBN 1 902646 47 9	PB
250 x 199mm	140pp	£9.99	1st edition

To order, visit www.lawpack.co.uk or call 020 7394 4040